Bible Stories for Teens

Christian Lessons, Biblical Truths, and Prayers to Help Teenagers Grow Strong in Faith

Table of Contents

Introduction

If you're holding this book in your hands, I want you to know something really important right from the start: It has been written for teen readers just like you!

Maybe you've tried reading the Bible before and didn't know where to start, or wondered: What is the most important thing I need to learn from a story I have just read?

As the author of this book, I want you to know: I get it. Sometimes, we grow up with adults or other authority figures telling us what to believe, but without any context – it's like learning a science formula but without the why or how.

Yet, the Bible is a Holy Book filled with incredible stories divinely inspired to provide us with guidance for everyday life. Stories of creation and how it still relates to us today, scripture of how people persevered during tough times, and how, even when things look bleak.

The selection of Bible stories that you are about to read have been lovingly curated to help you in your journey of growing in faith and growing closer to God. It includes true life recollections of everyday people. Those that doubted, messed up, ran from God, felt afraid, got rejected, had anxiety, and faced temptation.

But, as you will see in this collection of quick-read stories, God never gave up on them. Just like He will never give up on us. So, get ready to revisit incredible stories, what they mean for us today, and how they connect to modern life.

Get ready for bonus content too!

Inside this book, I've included:

- **Short, powerful lessons** that fit into your schedule.
- **Real prayers** you can say out loud or in your heart.
- **Big questions** to help you think about what you believe.
- **Truth** you can stand on when life gets messy.

Be sure to read until the end, as there is a bonus study track for when you would like to go deeper into the history of Bible stories and heroes.

Get ready to discover and learn incredible Bible truths in every story. Enjoy this beautiful volume, may you treasure it for years to come!

Part 1: Finding Your Identity in God (Genesis – Exodus)

Who are you really?

That's a question a lot of us ask, especially when life feels confusing or when we're trying to figure out who we're supposed to be. The truth is, the Bible starts by answering that very question!

In this section, you'll meet the first people God created, and others who were far from perfect. Yet, they were still deeply loved and chosen by Him. You'll read about Adam, Enoch, Noah, Abraham, Jacob, Joseph, and Moses. Each of their stories is different, but they all show us something important: Your true identity isn't found in what others say, what you've done, or even how you feel about yourself. Your identity is found in your Heavenly Creator who made you, sees you, and calls you by name.

Whether you're strong like Noah, afraid like Abraham, struggling like Jacob, or unsure like Moses, God has a purpose for you.

Chapter 1: Creation — Made for a Reason

The Bible Story (Genesis 1-2, Retold)

In the very beginning, there was nothing but darkness and emptiness.

Then God spoke. He said, "Let there be light," and **boom!** – there was light.

He made the oceans and the mountains, the trees and the flowers, the birds in the sky and the fish in the sea.

God did not create people with a word. He formed the man from dust and gave him breath (Genesis 2:7). He built the woman from the man's side (Genesis 2:22). This was not casual. It was direct and intentional.

God called the whole creation "very good" only after it was finished (Genesis 1:31). That statement was about the completed order, not about Adam and Eve alone.

Humans were made in the image of God (Genesis 1:27). That means they were created to reflect His authority, reason, and purpose. It means bearing weight, not chasing worth.

You were made to reflect God, not to impress the world. Your purpose is not to feel special. Your purpose is to live under His design. That is enough.

Takeaway: You Were Created For A Special Purpose

Sometimes the world can make you feel like you have to prove yourself. You might think:

"If I could just be more popular...

If I could just get better grades...

If I could just fit in... then maybe I'd matter."

But the truth is, you are in the right place at the right time because of **Who** made you.

God created you on purpose, with a purpose. You were created by the same God who painted the skies and carved out oceans. He sees the potential in you, even when you don't. You are **called, seen and loved**. And you are made to live a life that reflects His love and light in ways only you can.

Reflection Questions

- When have you felt like you didn't matter, or like you had to earn your worth?

- What do you call 'very good' in your life? Is it a thing? A Person? How do you treat the things you call very good?

- If you are created on purpose, for a purpose, what might that mean for how you live today?

(Write your thoughts below, share them with someone you trust, or simply take a few quiet moments to reflect.)

_____

_____

_____

_____

_____

_____

Prayer

God,

Thank You for making me on purpose.

When I feel small or invisible, remind me that You see me.

Help me believe that I am Your masterpiece.

Show me the plans You have for my life.

I want to walk with You every day.

Amen.

Faith Challenge

Today, whenever you look in the mirror, say this out loud:

"I am made by God. I am very good."

Say it even if you don't feel it yet.

Say it until your heart starts to believe it.

You were made for a reason. Never forget it.

Chapter 2: Enoch Walks with God — A Quiet Life That Pleased God

The Bible tells us about a man named Enoch, someone who stood out in a way the world often misses: He simply walked with God.

Let's take a look at his story.

The Bible Story (Genesis 5:21–24, Retold)

Enoch lived in the early generations after creation. Like the others in his line, he lived many years, but with one clear difference.

Scripture says, "Enoch walked with God" (Genesis 5:22). And then, "he was not, for God took him" (Genesis 5:24). There is no mention of death.

Hebrews 11:5 explains it further: "By faith Enoch was taken up so that he should not see death, and he was not found, because God had taken him." His removal was not ordinary. It was an exception, made by God, recorded without detail, and never repeated in the same way.

What set Enoch apart was not his age, but his walk. He lived in step with God, faithfully. That is what the record tells us.

Enoch left no speech, no monument, no kingdom. But his faith was remembered. Thousands of years later, his name still stands for one thing: obedience.

Takeaway: You Don't Have to Be Loud to Live Meaningfully

Enoch's story is proof that you just need to **walk with God** with steady trust, quiet faith, and a heart that stays close to Him. In today's world, it's easy to think that louder is better, that influence only comes from platforms, followers, or applause.

But God sees something deeper. He sees your small, daily choices. He sees your faith when no one else is watching. He hears your whispered prayers. He notices when you choose kindness over attention, obedience over popularity, and truth over trends.

God treasures the faithful and uses the simple, humble lives of people like Enoch, and you, to show the world what real faith looks like.

Reflection Questions

- What do you think faithfulness in God looks like today?
- What's one small, quiet habit, such as prayer, gratitude, or reading Scripture, that could help you stay close to Him this week?

(Write or reflect in your own way. God speaks even in stillness.)

_____

_____

_____

_____

_____

_____

_____

Prayer

God,

Sometimes I feel like I'm not doing enough.

But Enoch's story reminds me that just walking with You is powerful.

Help me trust that my quiet faith matters.

Help me stay close to You, even when no one's watching.

I want to walk with You every day.

Amen.

Faith Challenge

Today, take a 10-minute walk, just you and God.

Leave your phone behind.

As you walk, pray quietly.

You don't need fancy words.

Just talk to God like a friend.

And then listen.

Sometimes, the most powerful steps are the quiet ones.

Chapter 3: Noah — Trust in the Storm

Have you ever felt like you're the only one standing up for something right? Like everyone around you is doing one thing, but deep down, you know it's not right? It's hard to be the only one.

But there's a story about a man who stood alone and trusted God through the biggest storm the world had ever seen. Let's read more about Noah.

The Bible Story (Genesis 6–9, Retold)

The Bible says that generations after Adam and Eve, the world became corrupt. Cain murdered his brother. Violence spread. People ignored God and followed their own desires.

"Every intention of the thoughts of man's heart was only evil continually" (Genesis 6:5). God saw it. And He judged it.

The Lord said, "I will blot out man whom I have created from the face of the land" (Genesis 6:7). The flood was not a reset. It was judgment.

But one man found favor.

Noah walked with God (Genesis 6:9). While the rest of the world ignored truth, Noah listened. God gave him a command: build an ark. A flood was coming, and only those inside would be saved.

God told Noah to bring two of every unclean animal and seven pairs of every clean animal, and birds too (Genesis 7:2–3). This wasn't a myth. It was a command with structure and purpose.

Noah obeyed. He built the ark. He prepared. And when the waters came, everything outside was destroyed. Only Noah, his family, and those with him in the ark survived.

After the flood, God established a covenant. He set a rainbow in the sky as a sign of His promise: never again would He destroy the earth with a flood (Genesis 9:13–15).

God did what He said. He always does.

Takeaway: Trust Even When It Doesn't Make Sense

Sometimes doing the right thing feels lonely, and trusting God might feel risky. But remember this: God sees everything. He has a plan even when you don't understand it yet.

When you stand alone for what's right, you're never alone. God is standing with you, and when the storm hits, He is always your shelter.

Trust Him. Even when it's hard. Even when it's scary or it feels like no one else gets it. Because God always keeps His promises.

Reflection Questions

- When have you felt like the only one standing for something right?
- What aspects of God in Noah's story makes him trustworthy?

Prayer

God,

Help me trust You, even when it's hard.

Give me courage when I feel alone.

Remind me that You are with me, even when no one else is.

Build my faith like You built the ark: Strong enough to handle any storm.

Amen.

Faith Challenge

Pick one small thing today where you can trust God more.

It could be choosing kindness when others aren't, being honest, even if it's hard, or praying about something scary instead of worrying.

Whatever it is, take that one step. Trust Him with it. You're building something stronger than an ark: A life of faith.

Chapter 4: Abraham — Following When You're Afraid

Have you ever had to step into something completely new without knowing how it would turn out, such as a new school or trying out for a sports team?

It's scary to take a step when you can't see the whole road ahead, but that's exactly the kind of faith God calls us to. That's what Abraham had to learn.

The Bible Story (Genesis 12-21, Retold)

Abram lived in the city of Ur. He had land, family, and a stable life. Then God gave him a command: leave your country, your relatives, and your father's house, and go to the land that I will show you (Genesis 12:1). God promised to make Abram into a great nation, to bless him, and to make his name great so that he would be a blessing (Genesis 12:2).

Abram obeyed. He left everything and followed. As he traveled, God spoke again. But Abram and his wife Sarai remained childless. The promise stood, but the evidence did not appear. Then God brought Abram outside and said, "Look toward heaven, and number the stars, if you are able to number them. So shall your offspring be" (Genesis 15:5).

God made a covenant with Abram. He believed the Lord, and it was counted to him as righteousness (Genesis 15:6).

Time passed. God did not forget. He changed Abram's name to Abraham, meaning "father of many" (Genesis 17:5). He also changed Sarai's name to Sarah (Genesis 17:15).

Then the Lord did what He had said. Sarah gave birth to a son, Isaac (Genesis 21:1–3). Not because they understood. Not because they were strong. But because God always keeps His word.

Abraham's story is about trust. Trust when the outcome is not visible. Trust when nothing makes sense. Faith is not theory. It is action.

Takeaway: Faith Is Following Before You See

Faith is not about knowing the outcome. It is about trusting the One who commands. When God called Abraham, He did not reveal the full plan. He gave a command, and Abraham obeyed (Genesis 12:1–4).

God does not ask for achievement. He requires trust. Obedience matters more than understanding. Faith walks forward even when the path is unclear.

Reflection Questions

- How has this story helped you to better understand what it means to trust God?
- What's one area of your life where God might be asking you to trust Him more today?

Prayer

God,

Sometimes I'm scared to take steps when I can't see where they lead.

Help me trust You like Abraham did.

Help me follow even when it feels uncertain.

I believe You have good plans for me.

Give me courage to walk by faith, not just by sight.

Amen.

Faith Challenge

Think of one area where you're feeling unsure or afraid right now, such as a decision or a change you need to make. Pray about it, asking God to lead you step-by-step. Then, move forward in faith today. Trust that God is already ahead of you, making a way.

Chapter 5: Jacob Wrestles with God — Becoming Who You're Meant to Be

Have you ever felt stuck between who you are and who you want to be? Have you made mistakes you're not proud of, or are you scared of what lies ahead?

It sounds like you have a lot in common with Jacob. He was caught between a messy past and an unknown future. Luckily, in the middle of the night, something surprising happened that would change Jacob's future.

Jacob wrestled with God, and in that moment of struggle, everything changed.

The Bible Story (Genesis 32:22–31, Retold)

Jacob was going home. He was also going to face Esau, the brother he had deceived. Years earlier, Jacob had taken both the birthright and the blessing that belonged to Esau. He had lived by grasping, bargaining, and fleeing.

Now Esau was approaching with four hundred men. Jacob feared the worst. He sent his family across the river and stayed behind alone.

That night, a man came and wrestled with him until daybreak. They struggled without rest. When the man said, "Let me go," Jacob answered, "I will not let you go unless you bless me" (Genesis 32:26).

The man asked his name. Jacob answered. Then the man said, "Your name shall no longer be called Jacob, but Israel, for you have striven with God and with men, and have prevailed" (Genesis 32:28).

Jacob understood that he had encountered more than a man. He had wrestled with God. He limped away with a new name, a changed posture, and a memory of struggle.

The covenant had already been spoken at Bethel (Genesis 28). This was not a new promise. It was a turning point. Not a blessing earned, but an identity given.

Takeaway: God Meets You in the Struggle

Sometimes, we think we need to be perfect for God to bless us. But Jacob's story says the opposite. God met Jacob in the middle of fear, guilt, and struggle, and that's where God often meets us too.

God didn't reject Jacob. He renamed him, and He can do the same for you.

Reflection Questions

- What are you wrestling with right now? Is it fear, guilt, pressure, confusion?
- How might God be using your struggle to help you grow?
- What name would you want God to speak over your life? Brave, forgiven, chosen?

Prayer

God,

Sometimes I feel stuck.

I wrestle with fear, regret, and doubt.

But I believe You meet me in the struggle.

Change my heart.

Help me become who You made me to be.

Amen.

Faith Challenge

Write down one thing you're wrestling with, then bring it to God in prayer.

Say this out loud: "God, I won't let go until You bless me."

Trust that He hears you and that on the other side of the struggle is something new.

Chapter 6: Joseph — Trusting God's Plan Through Pain

Have you ever had a time when everything seemed to fall apart? Perhaps you had an argument with your best friend, or someone blamed you for something that wasn't your fault at all.

Maybe your dreams felt crushed, and you wondered, *"Where is God in all of this?"* Pain can make it feel like God has left you, but so often, the hardest moments are where His biggest plans begin. No one knew that better than Joseph.

The Bible Story (Genesis 37-50, Retold)

Joseph grew up in a big family with eleven brothers, and he was clearly his father's favorite. His dad even gave him a special colorful coat to show it.

Naturally, his brothers were jealous. One day, they'd had enough. They threw Joseph into a pit and sold him to slave traders. They took Joseph's robe, tore it, and dipped it in animal blood. When they brought it back to their father, he believed Joseph had been killed by a wild animal.

Meanwhile, Joseph was taken far away to Egypt. Yet, even there, God was with him. He worked hard as a servant in the house of a powerful man named Potiphar and earned his trust. But just when things seemed to be turning around, Potiphar's wife told a terrible lie. She accused Joseph of trying to hurt her, even though he had done nothing wrong. Joseph was thrown into prison for a crime he didn't commit.

Still, Joseph didn't give up. He kept trusting God. He interpreted dreams for two of Pharaoh's officials: The king's cupbearer and baker who had been thrown into jail. He explained exactly what their dreams meant, and just as he said, one of them was released and restored to his job.

When Pharaoh himself had disturbing dreams that no one could explain, the cupbearer remembered Joseph. Joseph was brought from prison to the palace. With God's help, he interpreted Pharaoh's dreams, warning of seven years of plenty followed by seven years of famine.

Pharaoh was so amazed, he made Joseph second-in-command over all of Egypt. Then, when the famine hit, people came from all over looking for food, including Joseph's brothers. They didn't recognize him at first. But instead of getting revenge, Joseph forgave them. He helped them and saved his whole family.

Joseph's pain wasn't the end of the story. It was part of God's bigger plan.

Takeaway: Pain Doesn't Cancel God's Purpose

It's easy to believe that God is good when life feels good. But what about when nothing makes sense? Joseph's story reminds us that pain doesn't mean God has disappeared.

It means God is **preparing something deeper**.

Joseph was sold by his brothers, wrongly accused, thrown into prison, and forgotten for years. But none of that stopped God's plan. In fact, God used every setback to lead Joseph into his calling.

When you're in the middle of heartbreak or confusion, it's hard to see the big picture. But remember: God is still writing your story, and he's still faithful.

So, if you're in a hard season, don't give up. You may not see it now, but God is inspiring you to grow strength, wisdom, and compassion.

Reflection Questions

- When have you felt like everything was going wrong, like God was distant or silent?

- What might God be building in you through a season of waiting, heartbreak, or confusion?

- How does Joseph's story help you trust God's plan even when it's not easy to understand?

(Pause. Reflect. Write. Pray. Let God meet you in the middle of the hard parts.)

Prayer

God,

Sometimes pain feels too heavy to carry.

Help me remember that You are with me even in the hardest times.

Use the things that hurt to grow my heart stronger in faith.

Help me trust Your plan, even when I can't see it yet.

Amen.

Faith Challenge

Think about something painful you've gone through or are going through now. Write down one way God might use it for good, even if you can't see it clearly yet.

Keep that note somewhere you'll see it often as a reminder: **God can bring purpose out of your pain.**

Chapter 7: Joseph Forgives His Brothers — Forgiveness Over Revenge

Have you ever been hurt by someone you trusted such as a best friend or someone you loved? When you're hurt, the easiest thing to want is revenge.

But Joseph's story shows a different way: the power of forgiveness. Let's continue where we left off in the previous story.

The Bible Story (Genesis 45, Retold)

The moment had finally come.

Joseph stood in front of the very brothers who had betrayed him, who had tossed him in a pit and sold him as a slave. Years had passed. He had been ripped from his home, thrown into prison for a crime he didn't commit, and forgotten by almost everyone. But not by God.

Now, Joseph was second-in-command over all of Egypt. His brothers had come, unaware of who he really was, desperate for food in a time of famine. Joseph had every right to be angry, every reason to say, "You don't deserve my help."

But instead, he revealed his true identity to his brothers. Yes, they had hurt him. Yes, their choices had changed everything. But Joseph saw something bigger. He saw God's hand at work.

He hugged his brothers. He wept. He promised to take care of them and their families. He didn't erase the past, but he chose to write a new future.

Joseph could have passed the pain on. Instead, he broke the cycle.

Reflection Questions

- When have you been hurt by someone and struggled to forgive?
- What would it look like to trust God with that hurt instead of holding onto revenge?

Prayer

God,

Forgiveness is hard.

Sometimes my heart wants to hold onto anger and pain.

Help me trust You enough to forgive — not because the hurt was okay, but because Your love is greater than the hurt.

Heal my heart.

Teach me to forgive like You forgive me.

Amen.

Faith Challenge

Think of someone you are struggling to forgive. Pray for them today — even if it's just a simple prayer:

"God, help them. Bless them. Heal my heart."

Forgiveness isn't always a feeling. Sometimes, it starts with a prayer — and God does the rest.

Chapter 8: Moses — Your Voice Matters to God

Have you ever felt like you weren't good enough to do something important? Maybe you were too nervous to speak up in class, or thought someone else was smarter, cooler, or stronger.

Maybe you wanted to make a difference but felt like your voice wouldn't matter. Moses felt the same way.

But God showed him, and can show you, that when He calls you, He also gives you everything you need.

The Bible Story (Exodus 3–4, Retold)

Moses was born a Hebrew but raised in Pharaoh's house. Though he lived among royalty, he saw the oppression of his people. One day, he witnessed an Egyptian beating a Hebrew. In anger, Moses struck and killed the Egyptian (Exodus 2:11-12). When the act became known, he fled to Midian.

In Midian, Moses lived as a shepherd. He married, kept flocks, and remained far from Egypt for many years. Then, one day, while tending sheep near Horeb, he saw a bush that burned but was not consumed. He approached it. God called to him from the fire (Exodus 3:4).

God said, "I have surely seen the affliction of My people... I have come down to deliver them... Come, I will send you to Pharaoh" (Exodus 3:7-10).

Moses hesitated. He questioned his ability. He asked what he should say and how the people would believe him. God answered each concern. He declared His name, gave signs, and promised, "I will be with you" (Exodus 3:12).

Moses was not chosen because of strength or confidence. He was chosen because God sent him. The mission was not about Moses. It was about obedience to God's command.

Takeaway: God Doesn't Call the Perfect — He Calls the Willing

You don't have to be the loudest voice in the room. You don't need to have all the right words, a polished story, or unshakable confidence.

When God called Moses, Moses didn't feel ready. He was unsure of his voice, nervous about speaking, and filled with self-doubt. He even begged God to send someone else. But God didn't give up on him.

Instead, He gave Moses exactly what he needed, including his brother Aaron to speak on his behalf (Exodus 7:1–2). Moses didn't go alone. God sent help.

God knows your fears. He knows your insecurities, and He still says, "I want to use you." Even if your voice shakes or you feel someone else could do a better job.

God isn't waiting for you to have it all together. He just wants your yes. When you trust Him, He fills in the gaps with strength, clarity, courage, and sometimes even people to walk alongside you.

You don't have to lead perfectly or speak flawlessly. You just have to trust the One who called you.

Reflection Questions

- When have you felt like you weren't bold enough, strong enough, or qualified?
- Is there a place in your life where God might be inviting you to trust Him?
- What would it look like to say, "God, I'm not perfect ... but I'm willing"?

(Take a moment. Breathe. Let your "yes" be the start of something big.)

Prayer

God,

Sometimes I feel small.

Sometimes I feel like my voice doesn't matter.

But You say it does.

Help me trust that You can use me, even when I feel weak.

Give me courage to say yes to whatever You are asking me to do.

Amen.

Faith Challenge

Today, if you feel nervous about speaking up, trying something new, or standing up for what's right. Take one brave step, even if it feels small. Trust that God is with you and that your voice matters. Every big story starts with one small yes.

Part 2: Courage When Life Gets Tough (Joshua – Esther)

What do you do when life feels too big for you? In this part of the Bible, we meet people who faced real fear, real danger, and real struggles, just like we do. They didn't always feel brave, but each one chose to trust God in the middle of it. From warriors like Joshua and Deborah, to unlikely heroes like Ruth and Esther, these stories show us that courage isn't about having all the answers, it's about trusting the One who does. The same God who gave them strength is ready to do the same for you.

Chapter 9: Joshua — Brave Steps Forward

Have you ever had a moment when you knew you had to do something scary? You knew you had to be brave, but being brave didn't mean you weren't afraid.

It meant you trusted something bigger than fear. Joshua knew that feeling, and he showed us how to take brave steps forward, even when the road looks impossible.

The Bible Story (Joshua 1–6, Retold)

Before Joshua ever stepped into leadership, God had already written a long story with His people. The Israelites had once been slaves in Egypt, but God rescued them through powerful miracles. He made a covenant with them, a promise that they would be His people, and He would be their God. He promised to bring them to a land of their own.

But after their rescue from Egypt, the people didn't trust God fully. They complained. They doubted. They disobeyed. And because of that, they wandered in the desert for forty years.

Now, that long journey was finally coming to an end.

Moses, their great leader, had passed away. God chose Joshua to take his place. Joshua had some huge shoes to fill. He wasn't just leading a group of people, he was leading a whole nation into the next chapter of God's promise. But there was still one big problem. The Promised Land wasn't empty. It was filled with strong armies, fortified cities, and enemies who weren't planning to move out.

God saw Joshua's fear and spoke clearly to him: "Be strong and courageous. Don't be afraid or discouraged. I will be with you wherever you go" (Joshua 1:9).

So Joshua chose to trust God, even when the next step didn't make much sense. The first challenge? The city of Jericho. A massive fortress with high, thick walls.

But instead of battle plans, God gave Joshua instructions that sounded more like a marching band routine. Walk around the city once a day for six days. On the seventh day, walk around it seven times, then blow your trumpets and shout.

It sounded impossible, but Joshua obeyed.

On the seventh day, when the people shouted, the walls came crashing down. Joshua won the battle thanks to making space for God's power to move.

Takeaway: God Is Faithful Even When We Struggle to Trust Him

The story of Joshua is a symbol of how God keeping His promises, even to a people who didn't always keep theirs. For generations, the Israelites had seen God provide. He rescued them from slavery and gave them food in the wilderness. Now, He was leading them into the land He had promised long ago.

God's instructions to Joshua were about trust. Would God's people believe Him enough to follow Him, even when it didn't make sense?

Joshua obeyed, because he remembered who God was: the One who had never broken a promise. That's the heart of this story.

When we feel unsure or unsteady, we can look back and remember all the ways God has come through. He's trustworthy.

Reflection Questions

- What is something in your life right now that feels scary, overwhelming, or uncertain?
- What would it look like to face that challenge **with God** instead of trying to figure it out alone?
- Is there one step you can take today that says, "God, I trust You"?

(You don't have to feel ready. You just have to be willing to move forward with Him.)

Prayer

God,

Sometimes I feel afraid when I face big challenges.

Help me remember that You are bigger than anything standing in my way.

Give me courage to take brave steps, even when the path looks scary.

Help me trust Your power, not just my own.

Amen.

Faith Challenge

Pick one challenge you are facing today.

Pray about it.

Then take one step of faith, even if it's a small one.

Maybe it's speaking up. Maybe it's choosing kindness. Maybe it's standing strong when others don't.

Your brave step opens the door for God to move.

Chapter 10: Deborah — Leading with Courage

Have you ever thought leadership was only for certain types of people? Maybe the loudest voice, the most popular person, or the strongest athlete? Maybe you've felt like leadership was for someone else, not you.

God often calls unexpected people to lead. People who are willing to listen to His voice, stand strong, and trust Him completely. Deborah's story shows that courage, not popularity, is what makes a real leader.

The Bible Story (Judges 4–5, Retold)

Long after Gideon's time, Israel faced another enemy: A cruel king named Jabin and his general, Sisera. Their army had **900 iron chariots**, which made them unbeatable in battle. The Israelites were suffering under Jabin's rule.

In the middle of this chaos, there was a woman named Deborah. She wasn't a warrior or a king. She was a prophet, someone who listened to God and shared His truth. She also served as a judge, helping people solve their problems.

One day, Deborah called for a man named Barak. She told him:

"The Lord commands you: Go, take 10,000 men and fight Sisera. God will give you victory." (Judges 4:6)

Barak was nervous. He said, *"I'll only go if you go with me."*

Deborah agreed. She wasn't afraid. Together, they led the people into battle. Just like God promised, Sisera's army was defeated, because God fought for them.

Deborah's courage and obedience helped save her people. She didn't lead by being the loudest or the strongest. She led by trusting God completely.

Takeaway: Leadership Is About Trusting God

Leadership in God's kingdom looks different. Deborah wasn't loud or pushy. She was **wise, faithful**, and **courageous**.

She listened to God, trusted His voice, and acted when others froze in fear. That's what made her a leader: Her trust.

If God is calling you to lead, even in a small way, that's enough. He doesn't expect you to lead in your own strength. He promises to go before you, beside you, and behind you.

True leadership starts with a "yes." It shows up in everyday choices, such as encouraging someone who feels left out, standing up for what's right, starting something that matters, or simply setting an example through how you live.

If God has placed a mission on your heart, don't hold back. He believes in you.

He'll equip you, and He'll be with you every step of the way.

Reflection Questions

- Have you ever felt too small, quiet, or unsure to lead, even when you sensed God nudging you?
- What is one area (at home, school, church, or online) where God might be calling you to lead with quiet courage?
- What's one step you can take this week to lead not from fear, but from faith?

(Leadership often starts with one brave yes. Let this be yours.)

Prayer

God,

Thank You for calling ordinary people to do extraordinary things.

When I feel scared or unsure, remind me that You are with me.

Help me listen to Your voice and lead with Your courage, not my own.

Make me bold for the things You ask me to do.
Amen.

Faith Challenge

Think of one way you can lead by example this week:

Maybe standing up for someone who feels alone.

Maybe speaking kindly when others gossip.

Maybe inviting someone new into your group.

Big leadership starts with small acts of courage.

Chapter 11: Gideon — God's Strength in Your Weakness

Have you ever felt like you weren't strong enough, smart enough, or brave enough to do something big? Maybe you looked at what God was asking you to do and thought, *"There's no way I can do this."*

Gideon felt the same way, but his story shows that when you trust God, **your weakness becomes the perfect place for His strength to shine.**

The Bible Story (Judges 6-7, Retold)

Israel again turned away from the Lord. They broke His covenant and worshiped idols. In response, God gave them into the hand of Midian for seven years (Judges 6:1). The Midianites raided their fields, destroyed their crops, and left the people hiding in caves.

Gideon was threshing wheat in secret when the angel of the Lord appeared and said, "The Lord is with you, O mighty man of valor" (Judges 6:12). Gideon did not see himself that way. He answered, "My clan is the weakest... and I am the least in my father's house" (Judges 6:15). But God said, "I will be with you" (Judges 6:16).

Gideon asked for signs. First, fire consumed an offering (Judges 6:21). Then came the fleece—wet one day, dry the next (Judges 6:36-40). God gave every answer.

When the time came to fight, Gideon assembled an army. But God said there were too many men. He reduced the army from thousands to three hundred (Judges 7:2-7). God did not want Israel to claim the victory by their own strength.

At night, Gideon and the three hundred surrounded the camp. They broke jars, blew trumpets, and shouted as God commanded. The Midianites fled in confusion. The battle ended before swords were drawn (Judges 7:20-22).

But the real point wasn't Gideon's bravery. It was about God. God used weakness to show His strength. He used a hesitant man to display His power. The victory was about reminding Israel that their God already was.

Takeaway: God Uses the Small and the Scared

You might feel like you don't have enough courage, strength or skills. But when you trust God, you have **more than enough**. God isn't looking for people who are already powerful. He's looking for people who are willing to trust His power. Your weakness is not a problem for God, it's an opportunity for His greatness to show through your life.

When you feel small, remember: **You plus God is always bigger than anything you face.**

Reflection Questions

- When have you felt too small or too weak for something big?
- How would it change your thinking if you truly believed God's strength could work through you?

Prayer

God,

Sometimes I feel like I'm not enough.

Thank You for reminding me that with You, I have everything I need.

Help me trust Your strengths instead of focusing on my weaknesses.

Use my life to show Your greatness to the world.

Amen.

Faith Challenge

Pick one thing today that scares you. Something you've been avoiding because you feel too small. Pray about it. Then, take one small step forward, trusting that God will meet you there with His strength.

Chapter 12: Ruth — Loyalty That Changes Everything

Have you ever had a friend or family member who needed you and you had to decide whether to stay or walk away? Choosing to stay loyal isn't always easy. It can mean sticking with someone even when it's hard. The story of Ruth shows us the kind of loyalty that changes lives.

The Bible Story (Ruth 1-4, Retold)

Ruth wasn't born into a family that worshiped God. She grew up in a land called Moab, where people followed different gods. But one day, Ruth married into a family from Israel, people who believed in the one true God.

Through them, Ruth got to know about God's love and faithfulness. Then disaster hit. Ruth's husband died. So did her father-in-law and brother-in-law.

All that was left were Ruth, her sister-in-law, and her mother-in-law, Naomi. Three women. Alone. With no protection, no money, no easy future. Naomi, heartbroken, decided to go back to her hometown in Israel. She told Ruth and her sister-in-law to go back to their own families, to start over. One sister-in-law left.

But Ruth refused. She said: **"Where you go, I will go. Where you stay, I will stay.**

Your people will be my people, and your God will be my God." (Ruth 1:16)

Ruth gave up everything to stay with Naomi. Life wasn't easy for them in Israel. Ruth worked hard gathering leftover grain from fields just to keep them fed. But God saw Ruth's loyalty, and He honored it.

Ruth caught the attention of a kind man named Boaz, who later married her. Together, they became part of the family line that would lead all the way to King David, and eventually to Jesus.

Ruth's loyalty didn't just change her life. It changed history.

Takeaway: Loyalty Reflects God's Heart

Real love doesn't quit when things get hard.

Real loyalty stays when it would be easier to walk away.

In a world where people are quick to abandon friendships, families, and even faith when it gets tough, God calls us to something deeper.

When you stand by someone with love and loyalty, you reflect the very heart of God.

God never gives up on you.

He is always faithful.

And when you stay loyal, even when it's hard, you show His kind of love to the world.

Small acts of loyalty can lead to bigger plans than you could ever imagine.

Reflection Questions

- When have you had to make a choice to stay loyal to someone, even when it was hard?
- Can you think of a time when something in your life felt broken or hopeless, but later, you saw how God brought something good out of it?

Prayer

God,

Thank You for never giving up on me.

Help me be loyal and loving like You.

Show me where I can stand by someone who needs me.

Teach me to love with a heart that reflects Your faithfulness.

Amen.

Faith Challenge

Think of one person you can encourage today by being loyal. Maybe it's a friend going through something hard or a family member who needs your support.

Reach out, help them, pray for them and show them they aren't alone. Loyalty isn't just a feeling. It's an action that changes lives.

Chapter 13: Samuel's Calling — Hearing God's Voice

Have you ever wondered if God actually speaks to people today?

Maybe you've thought, *"If God wants me to do something, how will I know?"*

Hearing God's voice can feel mysterious.

But the story of Samuel shows us that God still speaks — and He often speaks to young hearts who are willing to listen.

The Bible Story (1 Samuel 3, Retold)

Samuel was just a boy when God called him.

He lived in the temple, serving under a priest named Eli. But it was a spiritually dark time for Israel. People had turned away from God, and His voice had grown quiet. The Bible says that in those days, "the word of the Lord was rare" [1 Samuel 3:1]. Not because God had changed but because the people had stopped listening.

One night, as Samuel was sleeping, he heard a voice call out:

"Samuel!"

He jumped up and ran to Eli.

"Here I am! You called me!"

But Eli said, "I didn't call you. Go back to bed."

Samuel went back to sleep.

Again, he heard it: "Samuel!"

He ran to Eli again. "I'm here! You called me!" But Eli shook his head. "I didn't call you, my son. Lie down again."

This happened a third time. Finally, Eli realized what was happening: God was calling Samuel.

Eli gave him new instructions: "If you hear the voice again, say, 'Speak, Lord, for Your servant is listening.'"

So Samuel went back to bed. Sure enough, the voice came again: "Samuel! Samuel!"

This time, Samuel answered just like Eli told him: "Speak, Lord, for Your servant is listening" (1 Samuel 3:10).

That night, God spoke to Samuel for the first time, and many more times after that. Samuel grew up to be one of the greatest prophets in Israel's history. He anointed kings, spoke truth boldly, and helped turn the hearts of the people back toward God.

But it all started with one simple response: "I'm listening."

Takeaway: God Still Speaks, and He Wants You to Hear

God isn't silent. He still speaks to us today through His Word, through prayer, through wise people He places in our lives, and sometimes through a quiet stirring in our hearts.

But here's the truth: Samuel wasn't just an ordinary listener. He was called to be a prophet, a person God chose to speak through in a very specific way to lead His people (1 Samuel 3:20).

That role was unique, and not everyone hears from God like Samuel did. Still, there's something powerful we can learn from him.

Samuel was young. He didn't have everything figured out. But his heart was open. When God called, he didn't run or argue. He simply said, "Speak, Lord. I'm listening."

You don't have to be perfect or spiritually elite to tune your heart toward God. You just have to be humble and willing to respond.

Reflection Questions

- Have you ever felt like God was trying to get your attention?
- How can you make more space in your life to listen for God's voice?

Prayer

God,

I want to hear You.

I want to know Your voice.

Help me slow down and listen when You are speaking.

Teach me to follow wherever You lead.

I am ready to say, "Speak, Lord. I'm listening."

Amen.

Faith Challenge

Find a quiet space today, even if you have just five minutes. Turn off your phone, music, and distractions.

Pray this simple prayer: *"God, speak. I'm listening."* Then sit quietly. Don't rush. Sometimes the most powerful moments come in silence.

Chapter 14: David and Goliath — Be Strong, Even When You're Small

Have you ever faced something that felt way too big for you? Maybe it was a huge problem at school, a broken friendship, a dream that seemed impossible, or a fear that kept growing inside you. You looked at it and thought, *"I'm just one person. What can I do?"*

David knew what that felt like. But he also knew something bigger: That with God, you are never too small to make a difference.

The Bible Story (1 Samuel 17, Retold)

The army of Israel was stuck. Across the valley, the enemy army had a giant warrior named Goliath. He was over nine feet tall, covered in heavy armor, and had been fighting for years.

Every day, Goliath stood in the field and shouted: "Who will fight me? Send someone! If you win, we will be your servants. But if I win, you will be ours."

Everyone was terrified.

One day, a teenager named David showed up. He wasn't a soldier. He was a shepherd, a kid who spent his days protecting sheep from wild animals.

David heard Goliath's challenge, and he heard something else too: the fear in Israel's army.

David didn't see just a giant. He saw someone insulting God.

David trusted God more than he feared Goliath. He said to the king: "I'll fight him."

The king tried to dress David in heavy armor, but it didn't fit. David took it off and picked up what he knew best: his slingshot and five smooth stones. He stepped out into the field with only his faith and his courage.

Goliath laughed. But David wasn't laughing.

He said:

"You come against me with sword and spear, but I come against you in the name of the Lord." (1 Samuel 17:45)

David slung one stone at the giant. The stone hit Goliath right between the eyes. The giant crashed to the ground.

David won, not because he was the strongest, but because he trusted God with everything he had.

Takeaway: You Are Stronger Than You Think

David didn't win that battle to prove how brave *he* was. He stood in the gap for God's people and God brought the victory.

In the same way, Jesus stands in the gap for us. He doesn't just help us face our battles: He's already won the one we couldn't.

Where we were afraid, He was faithful. Where we were weak, He was victorious.

The story of David and Goliath isn't first about us being brave. It's about trusting the One who fights on our behalf.

Reflection Questions

- What's one "giant" you're facing right now?
- What would it look like to face that giant with **God's strength**, instead of relying on your own?
- What small, bold step could you take today to say: "I trust You, God, even here"?

(You don't have to feel brave to act in faith. Courage is showing up anyway, knowing God stands with you.)

Prayer

God,

Sometimes the problems I face feel way too big.

Sometimes I feel too small to make a difference.

Help me trust You like David did.

Give me the courage to step forward with faith, knowing You fight for me.

Amen.

Faith Challenge

Identify one "giant" in your life today.

Write it down.

Next to it, write this sentence:

"God is bigger than this."

Pray about it.

Then take one small action step forward — even if it feels scary.

You might be small, but you stand with the God who never loses.

Chapter 15: Elijah Runs and Hears God — God Speaks in the Quiet

Have you ever felt like running away from everything? Like the pressure is too much... the fear too big... and you're just done?

You're not the only one. Even Elijah, one of the greatest prophets in the Bible, reached a breaking point.

He had just seen a huge miracle, but then fear rushed in, and he ran for his life. What happened next is one of the most tender, honest moments in all of Scripture and it shows us something powerful about how God speaks.

The Bible Story (1 Kings 19, Retold)

Elijah was a prophet, a messenger sent by God to speak truth to a nation that had stopped listening. At the time, Israel was worshiping a false god named **Baal**, a fake deity people prayed to for rain and their crops, among others. Elijah stood almost alone in defending the one true God.

In a dramatic showdown on Mount Carmel, Elijah challenged 450 prophets of Baal. They called on their god all day and nothing happened. Then Elijah prayed once, and God answered with fire from heaven. Everyone saw it. The crowd fell on their faces in awe. It was a huge victory for God.

But not everyone celebrated. When Queen Jezebel heard what happened, she was furious. She sent Elijah a threat: "You're going to die." Elijah panicked. He ran for his life into the wilderness. Exhausted, he collapsed under a tree and prayed, "God, I've had enough. Let me die."

He felt completely alone. Afraid. Burned out.

But God didn't scold him. He didn't send a lecture or lightning. Instead, God sent an angel with food and let Elijah sleep. Twice.

Then God led Elijah to Mount Horeb, the same mountain where He had once spoken to Moses. There, Elijah hid in a cave. And God asked him a question, not once, but twice:

"What are you doing here, Elijah?"

Elijah poured out his heart both times: "I've done everything You asked. But I'm alone. Everyone else has turned away."

Then God told Elijah to stand on the mountain. A powerful wind tore through. Then an earthquake. Then fire.

But God wasn't in any of those.

Finally, there came a **gentle whisper**, a low, quiet sound. That's where Elijah heard God's presence.

God didn't just comfort Elijah. He gave him clear direction: "Go back. You're not finished yet."

God told him to anoint new kings, to find Elisha as his helper, and, most importantly, to remember that he was *not* alone. God had preserved 7,000 others who had stayed faithful.

Elijah's story reminds us: God's power doesn't always show up the way we expect. But His voice is never silent.

His mission for us continues, even when we feel like giving up.

Takeaway: God Doesn't Yell — He Whispers

Sometimes, we expect God to speak through big signs and loud moments. But more often, God speaks in the quiet. In the stillness. In the whisper.

Elijah feels alone but God points out that he's not. There are 7,000 others who have not bowed to Baal. This is important today too: our feelings of isolation may be real, but they're not always true. Elijah thought he was the last faithful one. But God showed him he wasn't alone, and neither are we. Sometimes, what we feel isn't the full picture.

Reflection Questions
- Have you ever wanted to run away from something hard?
- When was the last time you sat in silence and asked God to speak?

Prayer

God,

Sometimes life feels like too much.

I feel afraid.

I feel alone.

But I believe You are still here, even in the quiet.

Help me stop running.

Help me rest in You.

And help me listen for Your whisper.

Amen.

Faith Challenge

Find a quiet space today, no noise, no screens, no music.

Set a timer for five minutes.

Just sit with God.

Pray this:

"God, I'm listening."

Then let the silence stay.

God often speaks to those who are willing to wait in stillness.

Chapter 16: King Hezekiah — Praying When Everything Falls Apart

What do you do when the news is bad and everything feels like it's falling apart? When the odds are against you, the pressure is too heavy, and you can't fix it on your own?

That's exactly where King Hezekiah found himself. He had no backup plan, no power left to lean on. But instead of giving up, he did one simple, powerful thing: He spread it all out before God , and prayed.

The Bible Story (2 Kings 18-20, Retold)

Hezekiah was king in Judah. Unlike many before him, he trusted in the Lord. He removed the high places, tore down idols, and restored worship according to the law of God (2 Kings 18:3-6).

Then came Assyria. Their army had conquered every kingdom they faced. They surrounded Jerusalem and sent a message: do not think your God will deliver you. No other nation has escaped. You will fall next (2 Kings 18:28-35).

Hezekiah did not rely on military power. He went to the temple, took the letter from the Assyrians, and laid it before the Lord. Then he prayed: "O Lord, the God of Israel... You alone are God... Incline Your ear... deliver us" (2 Kings 19:15-19).

God responded through the prophet Isaiah. The message was clear: "Thus says the Lord... He shall not come into this city... for I will defend this city to save it" (2 Kings 19:32–34).

That night, the angel of the Lord struck down one hundred eighty-five thousand in the Assyrian camp. By morning, the army was gone. The siege ended without a battle (2 Kings 19:35–36).

Later, Hezekiah became sick. Isaiah brought a word from the Lord: "Set your house in order, for you shall die" (2 Kings 20:1).

Hezekiah turned to the wall and prayed. He wept. Before Isaiah left the courtyard, God sent him back with another message: "I have heard your prayer. I will heal you... I will add fifteen years to your life" (2 Kings 20:5–6).

Hezekiah's strength was not in himself. It was in the Word of the Lord. In war and in sickness, he sought God.

In every crisis, Hezekiah didn't rely on his own strength. He relied on the Word of the Lord.

Takeaway: When You Can't Win the Battle, Exalt the One Who Can

Sometimes, life brings threats you cannot outrun. Problems too big for your plans.

Moments too heavy for your strength.

But Hezekiah didn't just ask God for rescue. He exalted God's name.

He laid the enemy's letter before the Lord and said,

"God, You alone are King. You rule over every nation. Show the world who You are."

His prayer wasn't just about relief.

It was rooted in worship.

He wanted God's greatness to be known.

And God answered.

Not just because Hezekiah was afraid. But because Hezekiah remembered who God is.

When your strength runs out, that's not failure.

That's a moment to turn your eyes upward. Not just for help but for God's glory to be seen in your story. He still responds today.

Not always in the way we imagine, but always in the way that reveals who He is.

Reflection Questions

- What is something in your life right now that feels too big or too hard to handle?
- Have you ever tried laying it out before God in prayer, like Hezekiah did?
- What would change if your first response was prayer, not panic?

Prayer

God,

Sometimes I don't know what to do.

The fear is loud.

The pressure is heavy.

But I believe You are bigger.

So I'm laying this down before You.

Help me trust that You hear me — and that You're already working.

Amen.

Faith Challenge

Write down one thing that's stressing you out.

Then, like Hezekiah, physically lay it out before God — on your desk, your bed, or in your journal.

Pray over it.

Say:

"God, I give this to You."

Then leave it in His hands.

Chapter 17: Shadrach, Meshach, and Abednego — Faith in the Fire

Have you ever felt pressured to go along with something you knew was wrong?

Maybe you were afraid that if you didn't, people would laugh at you, leave you out, or even turn against you.

Standing strong for what's right isn't easy.

But the story of Shadrach, Meshach, and Abednego shows that when you stand with God, He stands with you, even in the fire.

The Bible Story (Daniel 3, Retold)

King Nebuchadnezzar ruled over Babylon, and he built a massive golden statue. He made a law: When the music played, **everyone** had to bow down and worship the statue.

Everyone. No exceptions.

But three young men, Shadrach, Meshach, and Abednego, refused. They worshiped the one true God, and they weren't about to bow to anyone or anything else.

The king was furious. He gave them a final warning: *"Bow, or you'll be thrown into a blazing furnace."*

Their answer was strong and clear:

"The God we serve is able to save us. But even if He doesn't, we will not bow." (Daniel 3:17-18)

Even if it cost them everything.

The king ordered the furnace heated seven times hotter than normal. The fire was so fierce it killed the soldiers who threw them in. But when the king looked into the flames, he was shocked.

There weren't three men in the fire — there were four.

One of them looked like "a son of the gods."

God was with them in the fire. And when they walked out, not even their clothes smelled like smoke.

The king praised their God: The God who saves, who shows up, who honors faith that stands strong.

Takeaway: Faith Stands When the World Bows

Shadrach, Meshach, and Abednego were not just resisting a trend.

They were defying a king.

In a foreign empire that had conquered their homeland, they stood before the most powerful ruler of their time. When commanded to bow before a golden image or be burned alive, they made their choice.

They didn't obey because they were sure God would deliver them.

They obeyed because they knew God was worthy—no matter the outcome.

Their courage was not rooted in comfort. It was rooted in conviction.

They knew that no threat from a king could overpower the truth of God.

God did not prevent the fire.

He entered it.

That is who He is.

He may not always remove the trial.

But He never abandons His people in it.

Their story reminds us: God's truth is greater than any throne.

His presence is stronger than any fire.

And His glory is worth every cost.

Faith that endures under pressure is not just noticed, it is honored. Because when you stand for what is right in the face of what is wrong, you echo the courage of those who trusted God in the furnace.

Reflection Questions

- Have you ever felt pressured to do something you knew wasn't right — just to fit in? What did you do?
- What would it look like to trust God boldly — even if it meant standing out or standing alone?
- Do you act in loyalty because of promise of reward or outcome or because it comes out of truth?

Prayer

God,

Give me the courage to stand strong when I feel pressured to bow to the wrong things.

Remind me that You are always with me, even when the fire feels hot.

Help me live boldly for You, no matter what others think.

Thank You for being the God who never leaves my side.

Amen.

Faith Challenge

Think about one area where you are tempted to "bow down" — to fit in, to stay quiet, to blend in.

Pray for strength today to stand strong, even if it feels hard.

Remember: you are never standing alone.

Chapter 18: Daniel in the Lion's Den — Trust When You're Surrounded

Have you ever felt trapped in a situation where doing the right thing seemed risky? Maybe you knew speaking up for your faith or your values would cost you friends, opportunities, or respect.

It's not easy to stand firm when you feel surrounded. Daniel knows exactly how that feels, and his story shows that even when you're surrounded by danger, **God is closer than you think.**

The Bible Story (Daniel 6, Retold)

Daniel had spent years serving as a leader in Babylon. He was known for being wise, honest, and faithful.

Even when he lived far from his home and among people who didn't believe in his God, Daniel stayed true.

Some of the other leaders were jealous. They didn't like how much the king respected Daniel. So, they came up with a sneaky plan.

They convinced the king to sign a law saying that **for thirty days**, no one could pray to any god or person except the king himself. Anyone who disobeyed would be thrown into a den of hungry lions.

Daniel heard about the law. He knew the risk. He knew what could happen. But Daniel didn't hide.

He went to his window, just like he always did, and prayed to God openly. The jealous leaders caught him and ran to tell the king.

The king, who liked Daniel, was heartbroken. But the law could not be undone. Daniel was thrown into the lion's den.

The stone was rolled across the entrance. It looked like the end.

But in the middle of the night, God sent an angel to shut the lions' mouths. When the king rushed to the den in the morning, he called out: "Daniel! Has your God saved you?"

And Daniel's voice answered back:

"My God sent His angel, and He shut the mouths of the lions." (Daniel 6:22)

Daniel was pulled out, completely unharmed. And the king praised Daniel's God, recognizing His power and greatness.

Takeaway: Trust God, Even When You Feel Surrounded

Daniel's story showed us this: our hope is in the God who holds all power, sees every act of obedience, and walks with His people through every trial.

God's presence was with Daniel and His glory was made known because Daniel stood firm.

T

hat same God still reigns.

You may not face lions, but you will face moments that feel risky. In those moments, don't trust your circumstances. Trust the One who is worthy.

Reflection Questions

- Have you ever felt surrounded by pressure to hide your faith, change who you are, or stay quiet about what you believe?

- What does it look like to keep trusting God in moments when everything feels risky or uncertain?

- Is there a "lion's den" moment in your life where you need to remember: **God is with me here**?

(Your courage doesn't have to roar — it just has to trust. God handles the lions.)

Prayer

God,

When I feel trapped, scared, or surrounded, remind me that You are bigger than anything I face.

Give me the courage to keep trusting You, even when it feels dangerous or lonely.

Help me stand strong and know that You are with me every step of the way.

Amen.

Faith Challenge

This week, choose one small way to stand strong for your faith:

- Praying openly.
- Standing up for what's right.
- Choosing honesty when it's hard.

Every brave step strengthens your faith — and shows others the strength of your God.

Chapter 19: Esther — You Were Born for This Moment

Have you ever felt caught between wanting to do what's right and being afraid of what might happen if you do?

Doing the right thing can feel risky. It can feel scary. But sometimes, you are exactly where you are for a reason and your courage can change everything.

That's the story of Esther.

The Bible Story (Esther 1–10, Retold)

Esther was a young Jewish girl living in exile under the rule of the Persian Empire. Her people had been conquered, scattered, and were now a minority under foreign kings. They had no power. No homeland. No protection.

One day, the king of Persia decided he needed a new queen. Esther was chosen—not because of her background, but because of her beauty. She kept her identity as a Jew hidden, just as her cousin Mordecai advised. In a foreign palace, surrounded by wealth and luxury, it would have been easy for her to stay silent.

But then came a crisis. A powerful official named Haman convinced the king to sign a decree that would wipe out all the Jews in the empire. Esther's people. Her family. Her heritage.

Mordecai sent word to Esther: "You must speak to the king."

But that wasn't simple. In Persia, approaching the king without an invitation, even as queen, could mean death. Esther hesitated. She was afraid. But Mordecai's reply was clear:

"Who knows if you were made queen for such a time as this?" (Esther 4:14)

Maybe God had placed Esther in this exact position, at this exact moment, for a greater purpose. Esther prayed. She fasted. Then she stepped into the throne room, risking everything.

The king listened. The plot was exposed. The Jews were saved. But this story isn't just about Esther's courage.

It's about God's hidden hand—guiding, protecting, and preserving His people, even when His name isn't mentioned once in the book.

God kept His covenant. He protected His people and He used Esther to do it. Even when God seems silent, He was never absent.

Takeaway: You Are Where You Are for a Reason

Sometimes, God positions you in just the right place at just the right time even if it feels uncertain, uncomfortable, or unnoticed.

That was true for Esther, but over time, through prayer, waiting, listening, and trusting, she stepped into what God had prepared.

Her courage wasn't about a single dramatic moment. It was a slow, steady faith, a willingness to risk everything for the good of others and the glory of God.

You may not have a throne or a kingdom, but you do have opportunities.

God often works behind the scenes, just like He did in Esther's story. He's still writing stories today through people like you.

So, if you're in a hard place, don't assume it's pointless. If you feel unseen, don't believe you're forgotten. You are where you are for a reason.

God can use your faithfulness even if no one sees it but Him.

Reflection Questions

- Have you ever had a moment where you had to choose between staying comfortable or doing what was right? What happened?
- Where in your life right now might God be nudging you to be brave, speak truth, or take a stand?
- What challenges will you allow yourself to welcome and apply?

(God sees the full picture — and He put you here for a reason. Don't be afraid to be bold.)

Prayer

God,

Sometimes it's hard to be brave.

Help me remember that You have a purpose for where I am and who I am.

Give me the courage to stand up for what's right, even when it feels risky.

Help me trust that You are with me in every step I take.

Amen.

Faith Challenge

Look around your life today.

Is there someone who needs you to stand with them?

Is there a place where you could speak up for what's right?

Take one small brave step today.

You never know how much your courage could mean to someone else — or to God's bigger plan.

Part 3: Returning to God — Mercy and Second Chances (Job – Jonah)

Sometimes life breaks you. Sometimes **you** do something wrong.

Maybe it's a mistake you made, a dream that collapsed, or a time when you ran the opposite direction from what you knew was right. This part of the Bible is for those moments.

In these stories, we meet people who felt angry, afraid, unqualified, or completely undone. Yet, they were never abandoned. Job teaches us how to keep trusting when everything falls apart. Nehemiah shows how God helps rebuild what's broken. Jonah reminds us that even when we run, God runs after us.

This section is all about second chances, divine comebacks, and the truth that God's love doesn't give up when we do.

Chapter 20: Job — Faith in the Middle of Pain

Have you ever wondered, *"Why is this happening to me?"*

Maybe you worked hard for something and still lost. Maybe you prayed for something important and it didn't happen.

It's a hard place to be and it's easy to wonder if God sees you or even cares.

But you're not the first to ask those questions. Job asked them too, and his story shows us what real faith looks like when everything falls apart.

The Bible Story (Job 1–42, Retold)

Job had a good life. He was honest, kind, and faithful to God. He had a big family, lots of land, and many blessings.

Then, almost overnight, Job lost everything.

His animals were stolen or killed. His servants were attacked. His children died in a terrible accident. And then Job himself became very sick.

Pain piled on pain.

Loss piled on loss.

His friends came to visit him, but instead of comforting him, they told him he must have done something wrong to deserve all this. Even his own wife said, "Just curse God and die."

But Job refused to give up on God.

He didn't pretend everything was fine, he cried out. He poured out his sadness, his anger, his confusion. He asked the hard questions. He didn't hide his pain.

Through it all, Job never walked away from God. He kept praying. He kept wrestling.

He kept believing that somehow, God was still good even when he didn't understand.

In the end, God spoke to Job with a reminder of His power, His wisdom, and His love.

God restored Job's life, giving him even more blessings than before. But the real miracle wasn't the blessings. The real miracle was Job's faith that survived the storm.

Takeaway: Real Faith Holds On, Even in the Hardest Times

Faith is **choosing to stay close to God**, even when nothing makes sense.

Job's life fell apart. He lost everything: his family, his health, his home.

And he didn't stay silent.

He cried.

He questioned.

He struggled.

But he never let go of God.

That's what real faith looks like.

Not a perfect smile — but a decision to **cling to God through the pain**.

It's okay to wrestle.

It's okay to feel broken.

It's okay to not understand.

What matters is that you **don't walk away**.

Because even when it feels like God is silent, He is still present.

Even when everything hurts, He is still holding you.

And even when your heart is breaking, He is building something stronger within you — something deeper than surface-level faith.

Pain doesn't mean God has abandoned you.

It might actually be the place where your faith grows roots that hold, no matter the storm.

Reflection Questions

- Have you ever walked through a time when life felt unfair, painful, or confusing — like Job?
- During that time, how did you respond to God? Did you draw closer, pull away, or feel stuck in between?
- What would it look like to say, even now: "God, I don't understand — but I'm not letting go"?

(Let this be the moment you hold on. You're not alone in your questions — or your faith.)

Prayer

God,

Sometimes life hurts so much I don't even know what to say.

Help me trust You even when I don't understand what's happening.

Give me the strength to hold on to You in the middle of the storm.

Remind me that You love me, even when I can't feel it.

Amen.

Faith Challenge

If you're going through something hard right now, take a few minutes to write out a prayer to God.

Be honest.

Tell Him your real feelings.

Then, at the bottom of your prayer, write this:

"God, I trust You. Even now."

Keep that prayer somewhere close.

Every time the pain feels heavy, go back and read it again.

Let it remind you: your faith is bigger than your pain.

Chapter 21: Nehemiah — Building Dreams with God's Help

Have you ever had a dream or goal that felt too big to reach? Maybe it was starting something new. Fixing something broken. Helping someone when it seemed too hard.

You knew it mattered but you also knew you couldn't do it alone.

Nehemiah had a dream like that. Through his story, we learn that when God calls you to build something, He also gives you the strength to finish it.

The Bible Story (Nehemiah 1-6, Retold)

Nehemiah wasn't a soldier or a famous leader. He was a cupbearer, someone who served drinks to the king of Persia and made sure they were safe.

But one day, Nehemiah heard devastating news. The walls around Jerusalem, his people's city, were broken down. The gates were burned. The people who lived there were weak, scared, and ashamed.

Nehemiah's heart broke.

He cried.

He fasted.

He prayed.

Then, even though he wasn't a warrior or a builder, Nehemiah felt God calling him to do something about it. He asked the king for permission to go rebuild the walls. The king said yes.

When Nehemiah got to Jerusalem, he didn't find an easy job. He found rubble. He found enemies who laughed at him, threatened him, and tried to stop the work.

But Nehemiah didn't quit.

He organized the people. He gave them tools and weapons. He encouraged them when they were tired.

And in just 52 days — with God's help — they rebuilt the broken walls of the city.

Nehemiah's faith and courage turned ruins into strength.

Takeaway: If God Gives You a Dream, He'll Help You Build It

God often calls ordinary people to do extraordinary things. Not because they are powerful, but because they trust Him.

When God gives you a dream it's going to take work.

It's going to face opposition.

You might even want to quit sometimes.

But remember: God doesn't give dreams without also giving the strength, the courage, and the help to see them through.

You aren't building alone. God is with you every step of the way. Don't quit just because it's hard. Big dreams are always built one small step at a time.

Reflection Questions

- What is one dream or goal you feel God has put on your heart?
- What small step could you take today toward building that dream?

Prayer

God,

Sometimes the dreams You give me feel too big and too hard.

Help me trust that You will help me build what You have called me to start.

Give me courage when I'm tired.

Give me strength when I feel small.

Help me stay faithful, step by step.

Amen.

Faith Challenge

Write down one dream, goal, or mission you feel pulled toward, even if it feels impossible right now.

Pray over it today.

Then write one action step you can take this week, no matter how small.

Building big things starts with one small yes.

Chapter 22: Jonah — Running from God's Call

Have you ever known you should do something but ran the other way instead? Maybe you felt a nudge to apologize, help someone, or take a risk, but fear, pride, or comfort got in the way.

Jonah did the same thing, but his story shows us that even when we run, God doesn't give up on us.

The Bible Story (Jonah 1–4, Retold)

One day, God gave Jonah a mission: "Go to the city of Nineveh. Tell the people there to stop doing evil and turn back to Me."

Nineveh was a scary place. The people there were known for being violent and cruel.

Jonah didn't want to go.

So, instead of obeying, Jonah ran away. He got on a ship sailing in the opposite direction.

A huge storm hit the sea. Waves crashed. The sailors on the boat panicked, throwing cargo overboard to stay afloat.

Finally, Jonah admitted he was the problem. He told them to throw him into the sea to calm the storm. Reluctantly, they did.

The moment Jonah hit the water, the sea grew calm.

God, in His mercy, sent a giant fish to swallow Jonah — not to punish him, but to save him.

Inside the belly of the fish, Jonah prayed.

He cried out to God with a heart full of regret, and after three days, the fish spit him out onto dry land.

This time, when God said, "Go to Nineveh," Jonah obeyed. He preached to the people, warning them to turn back to God.

They listened and repented. They changed their ways, and God showed them mercy.

Jonah wasn't perfect. He struggled with anger, pride, and fear, but God still used him to make a huge difference.

Takeaway: God's Mercy is Bigger

God told Jonah to go to Nineveh — a brutal, violent city. He didn't run because he was scared. He ran because he didn't want them to be saved.

Jonah knew God was merciful. That was the problem. He didn't think the Ninevites deserved it.

So, he got on a boat in the opposite direction. But God didn't abandon Jonah.

He pursued him — not to punish, but to restore. Even in Jonah's rebellion, God was working.

Even after his resistance, God gave him another chance to obey.

That same mercy is offered to us. Maybe you've resisted something God asked of you. Maybe you've let bitterness, pride, or comfort guide your steps.

It's not too late.

God's calling may stretch you. It may challenge what you think people deserve. But it will always lead toward redemption — for you and for others.

God's mercy is bigger than your mistakes. Bigger than your opinions. And always worth saying yes to.

Reflection Questions

- Is there something you feel God might be calling you to do that you're avoiding?
- How has this story inspired you to look differently at forgiveness?

Prayer

God,

Thank You for never giving up on me.

Even when I run or hide, You keep loving me.

Give me the courage to say yes to the things You call me to do.

Help me trust that Your plans are good, even when they feel scary.

Amen.

Faith Challenge

Think about one thing you know deep down God might be calling you to do, big or small.

It could be helping someone, forgiving someone, standing up for something right. Pray about it today.

Then take one step toward obedience even if it feels hard. God's plans are always better than your fears.

Part 4: Encountering Jesus — Love That Transforms (Matthew-John)

When Jesus entered the world, everything changed. He didn't come as a king in a castle, but as a baby in a manger, quiet, humble, and full of promise. From that moment on, lives began to shift.

This part of the Bible follows the life of Jesus, from His birth to His resurrection, and shows what happens when ordinary people meet an extraordinary Savior.

Some were sick. Some were outcasts. Some were caught in sin. Others were just curious or confused. But every single person who encountered Jesus came away changed because He met them with truth, love, and compassion.

These stories remind us that Jesus still meets us the same way today: personally, powerfully, and full of grace. When you truly encounter Him, your life will never be the same.

Chapter 23: Birth of Jesus — Hope in the Hard Times

Have you ever known a moment when everything felt dark?

That kind of darkness is not new.

From the beginning, humanity chose rebellion. Sin entered the world, and with it came separation from God. Pain, injustice, fear, and death followed. Darkness became the condition of the human heart (Genesis 3; Romans 5:12).

But God did not leave the world in that condition. He made a promise. Through the prophet Isaiah, He declared that those who walk in darkness would see a great light (Isaiah 9:2). That promise was not vague. It pointed to a Savior who would undo what sin had broken.

The fulfillment came in Jesus Christ. His birth was not just a sign of hope. It was the arrival of the Light of the World (John 8:12). In Him, the darkness could not remain.

The birth of Jesus is not sentimental. It is necessary. Without Him, there is no rescue. Without Him, there is no peace. He did not come to make life easier. He came to save the lost.

The light still shines. Not because the world is better, but because Christ is risen.

The Bible Story (Luke 2:1–20, Retold)

A long time ago, in a land ruled by a powerful empire, the people of Israel were waiting. They were longing for the promised Messiah.

The One who would fulfill God's covenant, rescue them from sin and death, and bring lasting peace.

And then, in the quiet of night, in a small town called Bethlehem, that promise was fulfilled.

Not with royal banners.

Not in a palace.

But in a stable.

The eternal Son of God, fully divine, fully human, entered the world as a newborn child.

His parents, Mary and Joseph, had traveled a long way to Bethlehem because of a government census. When they arrived, there was no room left for them anywhere.

Only a stable where animals stayed. And there, in the humblest of places, **Jesus Christ** was born.

Mary wrapped Him in cloth and laid Him in a manger because that was all they had.

Nearby, shepherds were out in the fields watching over their sheep. Suddenly, the night sky lit up as an angel appeared.

The angel spoke:

"Do not be afraid. I bring you good news that will bring great joy to all people.

Today, in the town of David, a Savior has been born to you; He is Christ the Lord." [Luke 2:10-11]

Then, a multitude of angels filled the sky, praising God with songs of glory. The shepherds didn't wait. They ran to see what God had done.

And there they found Him — the promised King, lying in a manger.

They left rejoicing, spreading the news.

The hope of the world had come.

Not just to bring comfort.

But to bring salvation.

Takeaway: God's Light Always Breaks Through

If you're walking through darkness — doubt, depression, family hurt, or deep grief — know this: You are not forgotten. You are not beyond reach.

Jesus came for you and the light He brings is not temporary.

One day, that light will fill the whole world when Christ returns, wipes every tear, and makes all things new (Revelation 21:23-25).

The light wins.

Not because life gets easier. But because Jesus reigns — now and forever.

Reflection Questions

- When you think about the story of Jesus being born in a manger, how does it shape the way you view God's closeness to people who feel unseen or overlooked?

- Jesus came as both Savior and King. What does it mean to you personally that God's rescue plan began with a baby in a feeding trough?

Prayer

God,

Thank You for sending Jesus into a broken world to bring light and hope.

When I feel stuck in fear or sadness, remind me that You are near.

Help me trust that Your love is stronger than anything I face.

Fill my heart with hope today.

Amen.

Faith Challenge

Think of someone you know who might be going through a hard time.

Write them a short message of encouragement today — even just a few words like,

"You are not alone. God loves you."

Sharing hope with someone else can remind you of the hope you have too.

Chapter 24: The Woman Who Touched Jesus's Robe — Faith That Reaches Out

Have you ever been desperate for help, but felt too afraid to reach out? Maybe you thought, *"Why would God care about someone like me?"*

There's a story about a woman who reached out to Jesus in the middle of a huge crowd and it shows that even the smallest step of faith matters deeply to Him.

The Bible Story (Luke 8:40-48, Retold)

Jesus was on His way to help a very important man's daughter who was sick. The crowds were pressing in all around Him — pushing, shouting, grabbing.

In the middle of all that noise and movement was a woman who had been suffering for **twelve years**. She had a bleeding illness that no doctor could fix. Because of her condition, she wasn't just sick, she was considered **unclean** by her community.

She wasn't supposed to touch anyone and she wasn't supposed to be near crowds.

But she had heard about Jesus. She thought, *"If I can just touch the edge of His robe, I will be healed."*

She didn't want to make a scene and she didn't want to stop Him.

She just reached out quietly, secretly, desperate for hope.

When she touched His robe, instantly, her bleeding stopped. Her body was healed.

Jesus stopped. He asked:

"Who touched Me?" (Luke 8:45)

The crowd denied it.

Peter said,

"Everyone is touching You, Jesus!"

But Jesus knew. He had felt healing power go out from Him.

Trembling, the woman came forward and told her whole story. Jesus didn't scold her. He didn't shame her.

He said:

"Daughter, your faith has healed you. Go in peace." (Luke 8:48)

Takeaway: Even the Smallest Step of Faith Matters

The woman didn't have a perfect plan. She didn't make a big scene. She was hurting, tired, and probably felt invisible.

But she had just enough courage to do one thing: **reach out to Jesus.** She believed that even a touch could change everything.

And it did.

Jesus honored her faith and He called her "daughter."

You don't need a bold speech or flawless words to get God's attention.

You just need to reach out in faith.

A whispered prayer.

A quiet moment of surrender.

A small choice to trust.

God notices all of it.

He meets you in the quiet.

He sees what others miss.

And when you reach for Him — even shakily — He responds with healing, peace, and love that goes deeper than words.

Reflection Questions

- Have you ever felt too small, unimportant, or unworthy to bring something to God? What made you feel that way?

- What is one area of your life where you need healing, hope, or help — and what would it look like to reach out to Jesus with even a tiny step of faith today?

- What might change if you believed Jesus sees and honors even your quietest acts of trust?

(He's not looking for perfect strength — just a heart willing to reach.)

Prayer

Jesus,

Thank You for seeing my small, quiet prayers.

Thank You for caring about every part of my life — even the parts I try to hide.

Give me the courage to reach out to You, trusting that Your love is always enough.

Heal my heart.

Grow my faith.

Amen.

Faith Challenge

Today, take one small step of faith:

- Pray about something you've been too afraid to bring to God.

- Talk to someone you trust about a struggle.

- Trust Jesus with something you feel is too broken.

Even small steps toward Jesus are powerful.

Chapter 25: Jesus Feeds the 5,000 — Trusting God with What You Have

In the feeding of the 5,000, Jesus didn't just meet a need —He revealed His divine power and authority.

With just a few loaves and fish, He showed that **He is enough**. The miracle was about who Jesus is: the Son of God who satisfies completely.

The Bible Story (John 6:1–14, Retold)

Huge crowds were following Jesus. Everywhere He went, people wanted to hear Him teach, see miracles, and feel His love.

One day, a massive crowd — **more than 5,000 people** — gathered to listen. They stayed so long that it got late, and people were hungry.

Jesus asked His disciple Philip,

"Where can we buy bread to feed all these people?"

Philip panicked.

"It would take months of wages to buy enough food!"

Andrew, another disciple, spoke up:

"There's a boy here with five small loaves of bread and two fish. But what good is that for so many?"

It seemed like nothing. Way too small for the huge need.

But Jesus smiled. He told everyone to sit down. He took the boy's little lunch. He gave thanks to God.

And then He began to pass it out. The bread and fish multiplied. Everyone ate **until they were full**.

Afterward, they gathered twelve baskets full of leftovers.

Twelve baskets — from one boy's tiny lunch.

Takeaway: Jesus is Enough

The feeding of the five thousand wasn't about human effort. It wasn't about someone having the perfect plan or a generous heart.

It was about Jesus and who He is. When the crowd was hungry, it was Jesus who provided.

Not just with food for their bodies, but with a sign pointing to something deeper.

He is the Bread of Life: the only One who satisfies the hunger of the soul.

Reflection Questions

- When you think about Jesus being the "Bread of Life," what do you think that means for your everyday needs — not just physically, but spiritually and emotionally?
- How might trusting in Jesus as your true provider change the way you approach stress, success, or even your sense of identity?

Prayer

Jesus,

Sometimes I feel like I don't have much to offer.

But You remind me that small things become big when I trust You.

Take what I have — my time, my talents, my heart — and use them to bless others.

I trust You to multiply what I bring.

Amen.

Faith Challenge

Pick one "small thing" this week to offer to God:

- An encouraging text to a friend.
- A few minutes helping someone.
- A small act of kindness.

Trust that God can use it in ways bigger than you can see.

Chapter 26: Peter Walks on Water — Keeping Your Eyes on Jesus

Have you ever started something brave but then fear crept in and made you doubt yourself? Maybe you stepped out in faith, but once things got scary, you thought, *"I can't do this!"*

Peter knows exactly how that feels. His story reminds us that when fear rises, **the key is to keep your eyes on Jesus.**

The Bible Story (Matthew 14:22-33, Retold)

After a long day of teaching and miracles, Jesus sent His disciples ahead of Him, across the lake in a boat. Meanwhile, He went up a mountain to pray.

Later that night, the disciples' boat was far from shore. The wind picked up. The waves grew rough. They were struggling to move forward.

In the middle of the night, through the storm and darkness, they saw someone walking on the water toward them.

At first, they were terrified.

"It's a ghost!" they cried.

But Jesus immediately said: **"Take courage! It is I. Don't be afraid."** (Matthew 14:27)

Peter called out, *"Lord, if it's really You, tell me to come to You on the water."*

Jesus said, *"Come."*

Peter stepped out of the boat — and for a few incredible moments, he actually walked on water. But then Peter saw the wind. He felt the waves.

Fear gripped his heart and he began to sink. "Lord, save me!" he cried.

Immediately, Jesus reached out His hand and caught him. **"You of little faith," He said, "why did you doubt?"** (Matthew 14:31)

When they climbed back into the boat, the wind died down. The disciples worshiped Jesus, saying, *"Truly You are the Son of God."*

Takeaway: Focus on Jesus, Not the Waves

Faith doesn't mean you'll never feel fear.

It means you know where to look **when fear shows up**.

Peter stepped out of the boat with bold faith.

He actually walked on water because his eyes were fixed on Jesus.

But the moment he shifted his focus to the storm... he started to sink.

The same thing happens to us.

Life brings problems, pressure, anxiety, doubt. It's easy to look around and feel overwhelmed.

But Jesus invites you to keep your eyes on **Him**, not on the chaos.

He doesn't expect you to be fearless. He just wants you to trust that He's **stronger than the storm.**

And even if you start to sink, even if fear wins for a moment, **Jesus is right there.**

He reaches out, holds you up, and reminds you: **You're not alone.** You don't walk on water by being perfect. You walk by focusing on the One who makes the impossible possible — and walking forward with Him.

Reflection Questions

- Have you ever stepped out in faith but fear made you hesitate or pull back? What happened?

- What would it look like for you to keep your eyes on Jesus right now?

- What simple phrase or truth can you repeat this week when fear tries to speak louder than faith?

Prayer

Jesus,

Sometimes fear feels bigger than my faith.

When the waves of life crash around me, help me keep my eyes on You.

Thank You for reaching out to catch me when I stumble.

Grow my trust, steady my heart, and lead me step by step.

Amen.

Faith Challenge

Think of one situation this week where fear is trying to pull you under.

Every time you feel fear rise, quietly pray:

"Jesus, I trust You."

Take one small step forward in faith — even if your knees are shaking.

Chapter 27: Jesus Calms the Storm — Finding Peace Inside Chaos

Have you ever felt like life was spinning out of control?

Maybe you were hit with bad news you didn't see coming.

Maybe school, friends, family, and future plans all felt like too much at once.

Maybe you just felt trapped in a storm of worry and fear, wondering if it would ever get better.

In moments like that, it's easy to think you're sinking.

But Jesus shows us that even when everything around you feels like chaos, He is still in control.

The Bible Story (Mark 4:35–41, Retold)

One evening, Jesus told His disciples, "Let's cross to the other side of the lake."

They got into a boat and started sailing. At first, everything was peaceful. But then a furious storm blew in.

Waves crashed into the boat. The wind howled. Water started filling the boat fast.

The disciples — some of them experienced fishermen — were terrified. They thought they were going to die.

Meanwhile, where was Jesus? He was asleep in the back of the boat, resting on a cushion.

In a panic, the disciples woke Him up. "Teacher! Don't you care if we drown?"

Jesus stood up.

He spoke to the storm:

"Peace. Be still." (Mark 4:39)

And just like that, the wind stopped.

The waves grew calm.

The sea became still.

Then Jesus turned to His disciples and asked: "Why are you so afraid? Do you still have no faith?" The disciples were amazed.

Even the wind and the waves obeyed Him.

Takeaway: Jesus Has Authority Over the Storm

When the disciples found themselves in a storm, they weren't just afraid of the waves.

They were overwhelmed by the realization of who was in the boat with them.

Jesus didn't calm the sea just to soothe their fear.

He did it to show them something deeper — that He is Lord over wind, waves, and all of creation.

This wasn't just a moment of peace.

It was a moment of revelation.

The disciples asked, "Who is this, that even the wind and sea obey Him?"

The answer: the Son of God.

Storms in life are real — and sometimes terrifying.

But this story doesn't promise that storms won't come.

It shows us that Jesus is not just present in the storm — He rules over it.

His power is greater than chaos.

His voice still carries authority.

And His presence is not a maybe — it's a promise.

So when life feels out of control, don't just look for peace.

Look to the One who commands the storm itself — and obeys no one but God.

Reflection Questions

- What does it mean to you that even the wind and waves obey Jesus?
- When life feels out of control, how can remembering who Jesus is help you respond differently?
- Are there areas in your life where you've been asking for peace more than seeking the presence of Christ Himself?

Prayer

Jesus,

When life feels crazy and scary, help me remember that You are bigger than any storm.

Calm my heart when I feel overwhelmed.

Teach me to trust You, even when the waves seem huge.

You are my peace, no matter what happens.

Amen.

Faith Challenge

The next time you feel overwhelmed or afraid, pause for a moment.

Close your eyes and quietly say,

"Jesus, bring Your peace."

Picture Him standing in the middle of your storm, strong and steady, speaking peace into your chaos.

You are never alone in the boat.

Chapter 28: Jesus and the Woman at the Well — Fully Known and Loved

Have you ever felt like you had to hide parts of yourself? Maybe you've messed up and felt like people wouldn't understand.

Maybe you've carried shame, loneliness, or a secret you hoped no one would see. It's easy to feel like if people really knew us, they wouldn't love us.

But Jesus shows us something different. He meets us right where we are and He loves us completely.

The Bible Story (John 4:1–26, Retold)

One day, Jesus was traveling through Samaria — a region that most Jewish people avoided.

There was a long-standing divide between Jews and Samaritans.

They disagreed about worship, history, and identity. To many Jews, Samaritans were outsiders — spiritually and culturally.

But Jesus chose to go through Samaria.

Tired from the journey, He stopped at a well around noon — the hottest part of the day.

That's when a Samaritan woman came to draw water. It was unusual. Most people came early, when it was cool and crowded. But she came alone, likely to avoid being seen or judged.

Then something even more unusual happened: Jesus — a Jewish man, a respected teacher — spoke to her. He said, "Will you give me a drink?"

This wasn't normal.

Men didn't speak openly to women like this in public, especially not rabbis. And Jews didn't speak to Samaritans, especially not with kindness.

But Jesus didn't ignore her. He didn't reject her. He engaged her. As they talked, Jesus told her something no stranger could have known — that she had been married five times, and was now living with someone who wasn't her husband.

He didn't bring this up to shame her. He brought it up to show her: He knew her. Entirely.

But the point wasn't just that Jesus saw her. It's what He revealed about Himself.

He offered her "living water" — something more satisfying than anything physical.

She asked about true worship — where and how it should happen.

And Jesus said something incredible:

"The time is coming, and has now come, when true worshipers will worship the Father in spirit and in truth... I who speak to you am He" (John 4:23-26).

Jesus openly told her: **He is the Messiah.**

She left her jar behind and ran into town.

She told everyone what had happened.

And because of her testimony, many Samaritans believed in Him.

This wasn't just a personal encounter.

It was a moment of revelation — and it changed a whole community.

Takeaway: You Are Fully Known and Fully Loved

Jesus didn't wait for the woman at the well to clean up her past or fix her mistakes.

He met her right where she was — carrying shame, hiding pain, and feeling unworthy.

And still, He offered her living water.

Still, He spoke to her with kindness.

Still, He called her seen, known, and loved.

That same love is for you.

You don't have to hide your past.

You don't have to pretend everything is perfect.

Reflection Questions

- Have you ever felt like you had to hide certain parts of yourself — your thoughts, struggles, or past — from God or others? Why?
- How would your life change if you truly believed that Jesus already sees every part of you and loves you just as you are?

Prayer

Jesus,

Thank You for loving me fully, even when I feel unworthy.

Thank You for seeing every part of me and still calling me Your own.

Help me live in the freedom of Your love, without hiding or fear.

Teach me to love others the same way You love me.

Amen.

Faith Challenge

Take a few quiet minutes today.

Talk honestly with Jesus about something you usually try to hide — a fear, a mistake, a worry.

Then remind yourself:

"Jesus sees it all. And He loves me completely."

Let His love wash away your shame.

Chapter 29: The Good Samaritan — Loving People Who Are Different

Have you ever seen someone hurting and wondered if you should help? Maybe you wanted to, but you felt too busy.

Maybe you were scared to get involved. Maybe you weren't sure if they were "your kind of person."

It's easy to care about people who look like us, talk like us, or believe the same things we do. It's harder to love people who are different. But Jesus teaches us that real love crosses every line.

The Bible Story (Luke 10:25-37, Retold)

One day, a religious expert asked Jesus a big question: "What must I do to inherit eternal life?"

Jesus answered, "Love God with all your heart, soul, strength, and mind — and love your neighbor as yourself."

The expert, trying to justify himself, asked, "And who is my neighbor?"

So Jesus told a story. A man was traveling down a dangerous road when he was attacked by robbers. They beat him, stole everything he had, and left him half-dead on the side of the road. A priest — someone who worked in the temple — came walking by.

He saw the man. But instead of helping, he crossed to the other side of the road and kept walking.

Later, another religious man, a Levite, came by. He also saw the hurting man. And he too crossed to the other side and walked away.

Finally, a Samaritan came by.

Now, Jews and Samaritans didn't get along. They avoided each other whenever they could. But when the Samaritan saw the man lying there, he didn't think about the differences between them.

He didn't wonder if the man was worth helping. He felt compassion. He went to him.

He bandaged his wounds. He put him on his donkey. He took him to an inn and paid for him to be cared for.

Jesus asked, "Who was a neighbor to the man?"

The answer was clear: the one who showed mercy.

Jesus said,

"Go and do the same." (Luke 10:37)

Takeaway: What This Story Teaches Us

The Samaritan in the story crossed every barrier: cultural, religious, personal. He showed compassion when others walked by.

But this parable isn't just about being brave or doing more. It's about seeing that **we are the ones on the side of the road** — wounded, helpless, and in need of rescue.

And Christ is the One who stops for us. Jesus is the true Good Samaritan —

the One who shows mercy when we deserve judgment, who pays the cost to bring us healing, and who calls us to love others with the love we've received.

Real love doesn't come from trying harder. It flows from grace.

We love because He first loved us. Not to earn anything but to reflect the mercy we've already been given.

Reflection Questions

- Have you ever seen someone hurting, excluded, or struggling — but felt unsure if you should get involved? What held you back?

- Is there someone in your world who's different from you — maybe in background, beliefs, or personality — that God might be nudging you to love or serve this week?

Prayer

Jesus,

Thank You for loving me, even when I didn't deserve it.

Help me love others the same way.

Open my eyes to see people who need kindness.

Give me courage to cross lines and reach out with real compassion.

Make my heart more like Yours.

Amen.

Faith Challenge

Look around your school, your neighborhood, or your church this week.

Find someone who might feel alone, different, or overlooked.

Do one small act of kindness for them — a smile, a kind word, sitting with them, inviting them in.

Real love is seen in real actions.

Chapter 30: Mary and Martha — Choosing What Matters Most

Do you ever feel like there's just too much to do? Homework. Chores. Friends. Notifications.

Sometimes even good things can leave you feeling rushed and distracted. That's exactly how Martha felt when Jesus came to visit.

She was trying to do everything right. But her sister Mary chose something different.

And Jesus gently showed Martha, and us, what truly matters most.

The Bible Story (Luke 10:38-42, Retold)

Jesus came to the village of Bethany. He was welcomed into the home of two sisters — Mary and Martha.

Martha went straight to work. She was cooking, cleaning, and trying to make everything perfect for Jesus.

Mary, on the other hand, sat down at Jesus's feet and just listened. Martha was frustrated.

She came to Jesus and said, **"Lord, don't You care that my sister has left me to do all the work by myself? Tell her to help me!"**

But Jesus answered kindly:

"Martha, Martha... you are worried and upset about many things, but only one thing is truly needed. Mary has chosen what is better, and it won't be taken away from her."

Jesus wasn't saying that serving is bad. He loved Martha.

But He wanted her to see that her value didn't come from doing everything —

it came from being with Him.

Takeaway Lesson: You Don't Have to Do More to Be Loved

It's easy to believe the lie that being busy equals being important. That we have to keep doing more, achieving more, proving ourselves — just to be enough.

But Jesus invites us into something better:

rest, presence, and love that's already ours.

Martha was doing good things. She was serving, planning, making everything just right.

But in all the doing, she almost missed what mattered most: **being with Jesus.**

Mary wasn't lazy. She was intentional. She chose to sit, listen, and soak in every word from the One who loved her most.

Jesus didn't correct Martha because her work was bad. He corrected her because her **heart was distracted**.

Sometimes, the most powerful thing you can do is stop. Not to be unproductive, but to be **present.**

Jesus wants more than your checklist. He wants your attention. He wants your heart.

Reflection Questions

- Do you feel more like Mary or Martha in this season of your life — and why?

- What's one thing that tends to distract you from simply being still with Jesus?

- What would it look like this week to press pause and choose time with God over pressure to keep performing?

(You don't need to earn God's love. You just need to come close — and sit for a while.)

Prayer

Jesus,

I'm often like Martha — busy, worried, and distracted.

But I want to be like Mary — present, listening, and still.

Help me remember that You love me, even when I stop doing and just sit with You.

Teach me what really matters most.

Amen.

Faith Challenge

Pick one day this week to spend 10 distraction-free minutes with Jesus.

No phone. No to-do list.

Just sit, be still, and listen.

Read a short Scripture.

Then pray:

"Jesus, I'm here. I want to choose You today."

Chapter 31: Jesus and the Adulterous Woman — Grace Instead of Shame

Have you ever felt like your mistake defined you? Like people only saw what you did wrong — not who you really are?

Shame can make you want to hide, run, or give up. But when Jesus meets a woman caught in sin and surrounded by judgment, He responds in a way no one expected.

He doesn't throw stones.

He offers grace.

The Bible Story (John 8:1–11, Retold)

It was morning, and Jesus was teaching in the temple courts. A crowd gathered to hear Him.

Suddenly, a group of religious leaders pushed through the people, dragging a woman with them.

They threw her in the center. "Teacher," they said, "This woman was caught in the act of adultery. The law says we should stone her. What do You say?"

They weren't really asking because they cared about justice — they were trying to trap Jesus.

Jesus didn't answer.

He bent down and wrote something in the dust with His finger. The crowd waited.

Finally, He stood up and said, **"Let the one who has never sinned throw the first stone."**

Silence.

Then — one by one — people started to leave.

Until it was just Jesus and the woman. He looked at her and said, **"Where are your accusers? Has no one condemned you?"**

"No one, Lord," she said.

"Then neither do I. Go now and leave your life of sin."

Jesus didn't ignore her sin. But He didn't shame her.

He offered her something she never expected: grace.

Takeaway: Jesus Doesn't Cancel — He Restores

In a world that's quick to cancel and slow to forgive,

Jesus offers something radical: **grace.**

The woman in this story stood in front of a crowd ready to condemn her.

Everyone saw her failure.

Everyone wanted to define her by her worst mistake.

But Jesus didn't.

He didn't excuse the sin.

But He also didn't throw a stone.

He extended **mercy.**

He gave her dignity.

He offered a new beginning.

The truth is, we've all messed up.

We've all carried shame or regret.

But with Jesus, **shame is never the end.**

You are not the sum of your failures.

You are not trapped in your past.

Jesus doesn't define you by what you've done —

He defines you by **who you are to Him**: loved, seen, and worth restoring.

When others walk away, He leans in.

When you expect judgment, He offers healing.

Jesus doesn't cancel your story.

He rewrites it with grace.

Reflection Questions

- Have you ever felt ashamed of something you've done — something you hoped no one would ever find out?
- How would it change your view of yourself if you imagined Jesus standing with you and saying, "I don't condemn you"?
- Is there someone in your life — a friend, a classmate, even yourself — who needs grace instead of judgment?

(Grace is powerful. It heals, it frees, and it rewrites stories — including yours.)

Prayer

Jesus,

Sometimes I feel like that woman —

exposed, afraid, and unsure if I deserve forgiveness.

But You don't reject me.

You speak love over my shame.

Help me believe that Your grace is bigger than my guilt.

Teach me to offer that grace to others too.

Amen.

Faith Challenge

If you're carrying something heavy from your past,

take a moment today to lay it down.

Write it on a piece of paper.

Then tear it up — and throw it away.

Say aloud:

"Jesus, You forgive me. I don't have to carry this anymore."

Then walk forward in freedom.

Chapter 32: Zacchaeus — Seen and Changed by Love

Have you ever felt invisible? Maybe you've walked into a room and felt like no one even noticed you were there.

Or maybe you felt noticed — but only for your mistakes.

Zacchaeus knew exactly what that felt like. But Jesus shows us that no matter who you are or what you've done, **you are seen, known, and loved.**

The Bible Story (Luke 19:1-10, Retold)

Zacchaeus wasn't a popular guy. He was a tax collector — and not just any tax collector, but a chief one.

Tax collectors back then were known for being cheaters and thieves, taking extra money from people and keeping it for themselves.

Most people hated Zacchaeus.

They saw him as a bad person, a traitor, someone who could never change. One day, Zacchaeus heard that Jesus was coming to town.

He wanted to see Him, but Zacchaeus had a problem: he was very short. The crowds were so big that Zacchaeus couldn't even get a glimpse of Jesus.

So, he did something unexpected: he climbed up into a sycamore tree. From up high, he could finally see over the crowd.

As Jesus walked by, something amazing happened. Jesus stopped, looked up at the tree, and said: **"Zacchaeus, come down immediately. I must stay at your house today."** (Luke 19:5)

Imagine how shocked Zacchaeus must have been. Everyone else saw him as a cheat and a thief. But Jesus saw him as someone worth stopping for.

Zacchaeus climbed down quickly and joyfully welcomed Jesus.

The crowd grumbled: *"Why is Jesus spending time with a sinner?"*

But Zacchaeus's heart was already changing.

He said:

"I will give half of my possessions to the poor, and if I've cheated anyone, I'll pay back four times the amount!"

Jesus smiled and said:

"Today, salvation has come to this house."

Takeaway: God Sees Beyond Your Past

To the crowd, Zacchaeus was a traitor. A thief. A man defined by greed and betrayal. They saw his sin — and they weren't wrong.

But Jesus saw more than just what he had done. He saw someone lost... and someone worth saving.

Jesus didn't demand perfection first. But He didn't ignore sin either.

He called Zacchaeus by name, invited Himself in, and brought a grace that led to transformation. Zacchaeus didn't just feel noticed. He was changed. He repented.

He gave back what he had stolen.

Because encountering Jesus doesn't just lift shame, it leads to a new life.

You may feel like your past defines you. Like your mistakes have already written your story.

But Jesus came for people exactly like Zacchaeus, and like you.

Your value isn't based on your record or reputation.

It's rooted in the mercy of God who made you and the righteousness of Christ offered to you.

And when you respond to that call — like Zacchaeus did — everything can change.

Reflection Questions

- Have you ever felt like your past or reputation made it hard for others to truly see you — or for you to forgive yourself?

- How does it make you feel to know that Jesus sees everything about you — and still loves you fully, without hesitation?

- What might change in your life if you believed Jesus wanted to "come over" — to walk with you, just as you are?

(He's not waiting for you to get it all together. He's just waiting for your "yes.")

Prayer

Jesus,

Thank You for seeing me, knowing me, and loving me even when others don't.

Thank You that I am not stuck in my past.

Help me respond to Your love with a heart that is ready to change.

Teach me to see others with the same grace and hope that You see me.

Amen.

Faith Challenge

This week, do something that shows love to someone others often overlook — a kid sitting alone, a person others ignore, or someone who feels invisible.

Be the person who notices, just like Jesus did.

Chapter 33: The Lost Son — Always Welcome Home

Have you ever made a choice you regretted? Maybe you thought you knew best or you pushed away the people who cared about you.

Jesus told a story about a son who made huge mistakes — but found out something amazing: **No matter how far you run, God's arms are always open.**

The Bible Story (Luke 15:11–32, Retold)

Jesus once told a short story to teach a deep truth.

There was a man who had two sons. One day, the younger son went to his father and said, *"I want my inheritance now."*

In their culture, asking for your inheritance early was like saying, *"I wish you were dead."*

But the father agreed.

He divided his property and gave the younger son his share. The son packed up everything and moved far away. He spent all the money quickly on wild living, parties, and bad choices.

Then a famine hit. The son had no money, friends or food left.

He got a job feeding pigs — a dirty, disgusting job for someone from his background. He was so hungry, he wished he could eat the pigs' food.

Finally, he realized how far he had fallen. He decided to go back home, but he didn't expect to be welcomed as a son. He hoped maybe he could work as a servant.

As he got close to home, his father saw him and ran to him. He threw his arms around his son, and kissed him.

The son started to apologize, *"I don't deserve to be your son..."*

But the father interrupted.

He called for the best robe, a ring, new sandals. He threw a giant party. He said:

"This son of mine was dead and is alive again; he was lost and is found." (Luke 15:24)

The father never stopped loving him.

Not for one second.

The older brother wasn't happy when his brother was being celebrated while he himself had stayed home, worked hard, and followed the rules.

But his father gently reminded him: "You are always with me, and everything I have is yours. But we had to celebrate because your brother was lost and now he's found."

This story reminds us that God's love isn't earned. It's offered — freely, fully, and for everyone who turns to Him.

Takeaway: God's Love Never Runs Out

In Jesus' story, the son didn't come home proudly. He came home humbled, repentant, and aware of what he had done wrong.

But, his father didn't meet him with punishment. Instead, he showed compassion because his son had returned home with a changed heart — and the father was eager to forgive.

That's how God responds to us. He calls you to turn — to come home honestly, to repent, and receive the grace only He can give.

Reflection Questions

- Have you ever felt like you messed up too badly — like maybe you'd disappointed God or couldn't return to Him? What made you feel that way?

- How does it feel to imagine God running toward you, not to punish you, but to hug you and call you His child?

- What's one step you could take this week to return to God — whether it's through prayer, honesty, or simply saying "I'm back"?

(You don't have to earn your way home. Just come — He's already waiting with love.)

Prayer

God,

Sometimes I run away, thinking I know better.

Sometimes I make choices that leave me feeling lost and ashamed.

Thank You for always loving me.

Thank You for welcoming me back with open arms.

Teach me to trust Your mercy and live in Your love.

Amen.

Faith Challenge

If there's something you've been hiding from God — a mistake, a secret, a fear — talk to Him about it today.

Remember:

You don't have to clean yourself up to come home.

You just have to come.

God's arms are already open.

Chapter 34: Jesus Washes the Disciples' Feet — Serving with Love

Have you ever thought that being great means being served by others? Maybe you've seen people act like they're "too important" to do the small, messy things.

But Jesus showed something totally different: **Real greatness comes from serving others with love.**

The Bible Story (John 13:1-17, Retold)

Theis story begins the night before Jesus would be arrested and crucified.

He knew His time with His disciples was almost over. Every word and action carried weight.

Before dinner, something surprising happened. In those days, people walked everywhere — through dust, dirt, and animal-filled streets. By the time they arrived for a meal, their feet were filthy.

It was normal for a servant to wash guests' feet. But that night, no one had done it.

Then, Jesus, their Lord, their Teacher, the Son of God, got up. He removed His outer robe. He tied a towel around His waist. He poured water into a basin. And one by one, He knelt to wash His disciples' feet.

Even Judas.

Jesus knew Judas would betray Him. And still... He knelt before him. He served him.

It stunned the room.

Peter even tried to stop Him. But Jesus told him this had to happen. When He finished, Jesus said: "Now that I, your Lord and Teacher, have washed your feet, you also should wash one another's feet." (John 13:14)

He wasn't just giving them a lesson in hygiene. He was giving them a picture of the Kingdom.

Real leadership looks like humility. Real love looks like service, even when it's uncomfortable or undeserved.

Jesus showed them what it means to love with no strings attached. Then He told them:

Go and do the same.

Takeaway: True Greatness Looks Like Serving

When Jesus knelt to wash His disciples' feet, it was a glimpse of the cross. A picture of how He would humble Himself even further — giving His life to cleanse us from sin.

His act of humility pointed to something far deeper: We don't just need an example — we need a Savior.

But once we've received His grace, He calls us to reflect it, to love boldly.

True greatness isn't about being seen, it's about surrender.

When you serve others you're truly walking in the way of your Savior, who knelt low to lift us up.

Reflection Questions

- Have you ever had a moment where you served someone even though it was difficult, unnoticed, or inconvenient? What was that like?

- What's one small way you can serve someone this week — at home, school, or church — with quiet strength and love?

- What would it look like to lead by lowering yourself, just like Jesus did?

(Greatness in God's Kingdom begins with a towel, not a throne.)

Prayer

Jesus,

Thank You for showing me what true love looks like.

Thank You for not acting too important to serve others.

Teach me to be humble.

Teach me to love people the way You do — not just with words, but with actions.

Help me find joy in lifting others up.

Amen.

Faith Challenge

Find one way to serve someone this week —

- Help a friend without being asked.
- Do a chore without seeking praise.
- Write a note of encouragement.
- Pick up after someone else without complaining.

Every small act of service plants seeds of love.

Chapter 35: Crucifixion and Resurrection — Stronger Than Death

The resurrection of Jesus is the moment that changed everything. Jesus died for our sins, and when He rose, it proved that sin was paid for, death was defeated, and Satan had lost.

The resurrection is not the end of a sad story —it's the beginning of a new one, sealed with power, hope, and eternal victory.

The Bible Story (John 19-20, Retold)

Jesus had spent years teaching people about God's love, healing the sick, forgiving sins, and bringing hope to everyone He met. He lived a life full of truth, kindness, and courage.

But not everyone liked what Jesus was doing. The religious leaders felt threatened by Him. They were jealous, afraid, and angry. They plotted to kill Him.

One night, Jesus was arrested. His closest friends ran away, terrified.

He was put on trial, though He had done nothing wrong. The crowd — the same crowd that had once cheered for Him — now shouted, "Crucify Him!"

Jesus was beaten, mocked, and nailed to a wooden cross. He hung there, bleeding, while people jeered and soldiers gambled for His clothes.

Then, in deep pain, Jesus cried out: **"It is finished."** (John 19:30)

He bowed His head and died.

It seemed like the end.

Hope seemed crushed.

His followers hid in fear, broken-hearted.

But it wasn't the end.

Three days later, early in the morning, some women went to Jesus's tomb.

They found the stone rolled away.

The tomb was empty.

An angel told them the incredible news:

"He is not here; He has risen!" (Luke 24:6)

Jesus had defeated death.

He is alive.

Hope wasn't dead — it was stronger than ever.

Takeaway: The Cross Paid It All. The Resurrection Proves It.

Jesus didn't die just to show how much He loves you — He died to take your place. At the cross, He bore the full weight of our sins. He was pierced for our transgressions, and in His death, the debt was paid.

But the story doesn't end at the cross. Three days later, Jesus rose again as a declaration of victory.

His resurrection proves that His sacrifice was accepted. It means sin has been conquered, death has been defeated, and Satan has lost.

Now, for everyone who turns to Him in repentance and faith, there is forgiveness, freedom, and eternal life (Romans 10:9–10).

Jesus is alive — and He is Lord.

Reflection Question

- How does knowing Jesus conquered death itself give you courage to face what you're walking through?

Prayer

Jesus,

Thank You for loving me enough to die for me.

Thank You for rising again and proving that love is stronger than death.

Help me trust in Your victory when life feels hard.

Teach me to live every day with the hope and courage You give.

Amen.

Faith Challenge

Take a moment today to write down something you feel is "over" or "too broken."

Then, next to it, write this:

"Nothing is impossible with God." (Luke 1:37)

Pray over it.

Ask Jesus to bring new life where you feel stuck or hopeless.

Resurrection isn't just something that happened long ago — it's a power that still changes lives today.

Chapter 36: The Thief on the Cross — It's Never Too Late

Have you ever felt like you missed your chance? Like it's too late to fix what you've done, too late to change, too late for God to still care about you?

The thief on the cross thought his story was over. He had wasted his life and he was dying.

But in his very last moments, he looked to Jesus and discovered that grace still had room for him.

The Bible Story (Luke 23:32–43, Retold)

As Jesus was crucified, two criminals hung on either side of Him. One joined the voices of the crowd, sneering at Jesus: "If You're really the Messiah, save Yourself — and us!"

The other man responded differently. He wasn't just facing death — he was facing truth. He rebuked the first thief: "Don't you fear God? We're getting what we deserve. But this man has done nothing wrong."

In that moment, he saw something the others missed. He recognized Jesus not as a victim, but as a King. Not as a criminal, but as the righteous Judge.

And with nothing to offer — no way to earn grace — he turned to Jesus in faith and said:

"Jesus, remember me when You come into Your kingdom."

It wasn't a last-minute escape. It was a humble confession. A plea of repentance. A cry for mercy.

Jesus answered with a promise that reached beyond death: "Truly I tell you, today you will be with Me in paradise." No religious performance. No ability to fix his past. Just a repentant heart, real faith, and a Savior full of grace.

Takeaway: It's Never Too Late for Grace

God's grace isn't earned by good behavior or a perfect track record. It's offered through faith in Jesus, even at the final breath.

The thief on the cross couldn't go back and fix his past. He couldn't make up for the wrong he'd done. But in a moment of clarity, he saw who Jesus really was: The Savior, the Son of God.

In that moment, he turned to Christ in faith and repentance, trusting Him as Lord.

Jesus responded with a promise: "Today, you will be with Me in paradise."

This is a picture of what real saving faith looks like — a heart that confesses guilt, recognizes Jesus as King, and asks for mercy.

If you turn to Jesus with a repentant heart and trust Him fully, His answer will be the same: Welcome home.

Reflection Questions

- Have you ever felt like it was too late to turn your life around or get close to God again? What made you feel that way?
- What does the story of the thief on the cross reveal about Jesus's heart — especially for people who feel like they've failed?
- What would it look like for you to trust Jesus with **your whole story** — even the messy, broken, or unfinished parts?

(Grace isn't earned. It's received — and it's always waiting for you to say yes.)

Prayer

Jesus,

Sometimes I feel like I've missed my chance.

Like I've failed too much or waited too long.

But Your words to the thief give me hope.

You never give up on us.

Help me trust that it's not too late for me.

I believe You remember me — and that Your grace is enough.

Amen.

Faith Challenge

Write this as a reminder and place it where you'll see it:

"God still calls sinners to repent — but the time to answer is now."

Do not wait. Grace is real, but it is not endless on your terms. "Now is the day of salvation" (2 Corinthians 6:2). You are not beyond reach, but you are not promised another hour (Hebrews 9:27). Respond while the door is open.

Chapter 37: Thomas Doubts — When You Need Proof

Have you ever had questions about God? Like, "Is this even real?" Or, "Why doesn't He just show me something clear?"

You're not the only one.

One of Jesus's own disciples — Thomas — wrestled with serious doubt. But Jesus met him with grace.

The Bible Story (John 20:24-29, Retold)

It was just days after Jesus had risen from the dead. The disciples were gathered together — excited, confused, amazed. They had seen Jesus alive again.

But Thomas wasn't there. When the others told him, "We've seen the Lord!" he just couldn't believe it.

"Unless I see the nail marks in His hands," Thomas said, "and put my finger where the nails were... I won't believe it."

He wasn't being difficult. He just needed proof.

A week later, the disciples were together again. This time, Thomas was there. And suddenly, Jesus appeared. Right in the room with them.

He looked at Thomas and said, **"Put your finger here. See My hands. Reach out your hand and put it into My side. Stop doubting and believe."**

Thomas fell to his knees and said, **"My Lord and my God!"**

Jesus replied, **"You believe because you've seen Me.**

Blessed are those who haven't seen — and still believe."

Takeaway: Doubt Isn't the End of Faith

Thomas wanted to know that it was real.

He had seen pain, loss, and confusion. He wasn't ready to believe without something he could touch, see, and understand.

Instead of scolding him, **Jesus met him in his doubt.** He offered His hands. He invited Thomas closer. That's grace.

Doubt doesn't disqualify you. It doesn't mean you're a bad Christian. It means you're **wrestling honestly** with big questions — and that's part of real faith.

What matters is that you bring your questions to Jesus. Don't hide them. Don't carry them alone.

Jesus wants to walk with you through your doubts. He'll lead you to something deeper, stronger, and more personal than blind belief. He offers proof, presence, and peace.

Reflection Questions

- Have you ever had doubts about your faith — about God's existence, His goodness, or whether He's really listening? What was that like?

- If you could ask Jesus one honest question today, what would it be?

- How does it feel to know that Jesus didn't shame Thomas — He welcomed him with kindness and gave him exactly what he needed?

(Faith doesn't mean you never doubt. It means you bring your doubt to the One who understands — and stays.)

Prayer

Jesus,

Sometimes I wrestle with doubts.

I want to believe, but I also want proof.

Thank You for not pushing Thomas away — and for not pushing me away either.

Help me keep seeking You.

Help me believe, even when it's hard.

Amen.

Faith Challenge

Take five minutes to write out your honest questions for God.

Don't hold back — He already knows your heart.

Then pray this simple line:

"Jesus, show me who You really are."

Look for ways He might answer — in Scripture, in quiet moments, or through others.

Chapter 38: Peter Is Restored — When You've Messed Up Big

Have you ever made a mistake that you thought couldn't be fixed?

That's how Peter felt. He didn't just mess up a little. He denied even knowing Jesus... three times.

But after the worst moment of his life, something beautiful happened. Jesus came back for him.

The Bible Story (John 21:1–19, Retold)

Peter had once told Jesus, "I'll never leave You."

But on the night Jesus was arrested, Peter was scared. Three different people asked if he was one of Jesus's followers. And all three times, he said no.

"I don't know Him."

And then — the rooster crowed. Just like Jesus said it would.

Peter realized what he'd done. He ran away and wept bitterly. Days later, after Jesus had risen from the dead,

Peter and some of the other disciples went back to fishing. One morning, they saw someone on the shore calling out to them.

It was Jesus.

When Peter realized who it was, he jumped into the water and swam to shore. Jesus had made breakfast. After they ate, Jesus looked at Peter and asked, **"Do you love Me?"**

Peter said, "Yes, Lord. You know I do." Jesus asked again. And again.

Three times — just like the three times Peter had denied Him. But this time, Jesus wasn't shaming Peter. He was restoring him.

And then He said,

"Feed My sheep."

"Follow Me."

Jesus was saying:

I still believe in you.

I still want you.

Let's start again.

Takeaway: God Doesn't Give Up on You

Peter didn't just make a small mistake — he denied even knowing Jesus. Three times.

At the very moment Jesus needed him most. And yet...

Jesus didn't write Peter off. He didn't hold it over his head. **He came back to restore him.**

That's what Jesus does. He sees your worst moment, and still chooses you. Not to shame you, but to **rewrite your story.**

He looks for hearts willing to return.

Peter's failure didn't end his story — it shaped it. Through grace, he became one of the boldest leaders the Church has ever known.

So, remember:

You are not disqualified.

You are not too broken.

You are not your failure.

Jesus still calls your name.

And He still believes in you.

Reflection Questions

- Have you ever felt like you made a mistake too big to come back from — something that made you feel ashamed or unworthy?

- What would it mean to truly believe that Jesus sees your failure and still says, "I'm not done with you"?

- What's one step you can take today to walk forward in grace, not guilt?

(Jesus doesn't give up on you — and He's still writing your story.)

Prayer

Jesus,

I've made mistakes.

I've said things and done things I regret.

But You didn't give up on Peter — and I believe You won't give up on me.

Help me receive Your forgiveness,

and follow You with a whole heart.

Amen.

Faith Challenge

Take time today to write a letter — from Jesus to you.

Start it with:

"I know what you did... and I still love you."

Let those words remind you that your failure is not the end of your story.

Part 5: Faith That Changes the World (Acts – Revelation)

Jesus rose from the dead, but that wasn't the end of the story. It was just the beginning. In this section, you'll meet bold believers like Stephen, Philip, and Paul who carried the message of Jesus into the world. You'll discover the power God gives us to stand strong, speak truth, and share our faith. And you'll see how the story ends, not in fear, but in a future filled with hope. This is what happens when faith moves from your heart to your life: it doesn't just change you: it starts changing the world.

Chapter 39: Stephen Stands Strong — Faith That Speaks Boldly

Have you ever been afraid to speak up for what you believe? Being bold about your faith isn't easy, especially when people push back.

But Stephen was one of the first followers of Jesus who showed what true courage looks like. Even when it cost him everything, he stood strong because he knew who he stood for.

The Bible Story (Acts 6-7, Retold)

Stephen was one of the early believers in the church. He wasn't one of the twelve apostles — he was chosen to help serve the community, especially the widows and the poor.

But Stephen wasn't just a helper. He was full of the Holy Spirit. He spoke with wisdom, power, and love.

Some religious leaders didn't like that. They argued with him but they couldn't outsmart him. So, they spread lies. They said he was speaking against God.

They dragged him in front of a council and accused him. Even then, Stephen didn't back down. He stood up and told the truth about how the people had ignored God's voice and rejected Jesus, the Son of God.

It made the leaders furious. They rushed at him, dragged him outside the city, and began to stone him.

But as Stephen was dying, he looked up and saw something incredible: Jesus, standing at the right hand of God, watching him.

And Stephen prayed,

"Lord, don't hold this sin against them."

Just like Jesus, he forgave, even in the middle of pain.

Takeaway: Real Faith Remains — Even When It Costs Everything

Stephen's story is powerful and sobering. He didn't just believe quietly; he spoke boldly about Jesus, even when the crowd turned violent. He was falsely accused, dragged out of the city, and stoned to death. But through it all, he didn't respond with hate. He looked to heaven, forgave his enemies, and trusted Jesus until his final breath. Stephen reminds us that following Jesus is not about popularity or safety. It's about truth, courage, and eternal hope. When you take a stand for Christ, it may not be easy — but you're never alone. Jesus stood for Stephen in heaven (Acts 7:55–56), and He stands with you now. Faith that endures, even through rejection or suffering, points to a Savior who's worth everything.

Reflection Questions

- Have you ever had a moment where you stayed quiet about your faith because you were afraid of what others might think or say? How did that feel?

- What do you think gave Stephen the strength to stay faithful even when everything seemed to be against him?

- What's one specific way you could live or speak boldly for Jesus this week — with kindness, clarity, and love?

(You're not alone when you stand for Jesus. He's standing with you — and that changes everything.)

Prayer

Jesus,

I want to have faith like Stephen.

A faith that stands when it's scary.

A voice that speaks truth with love.

Give me courage, not to impress others,

but to honor You.

Stand with me — and help me stand for You.

Amen.

Faith Challenge

Think of one situation this week where you could speak kindly and clearly about your faith —

maybe in a conversation with a friend,

a social media post,

or standing up for someone who's left out.

Ask God for boldness.

Then do it — with love.

Chapter 40: Pentecost — The Power to Change the World

Have you ever felt too small to make a difference? It's easy to think you have to wait until you're older, smarter, or stronger to matter.

But the story of Pentecost shows that when God's Spirit fills you, you have everything you need to live boldly right now.

The Bible Story (Acts 2, Retold)

After Jesus rose from the dead, He spent time with His followers. He taught them more about God's Kingdom and gave them a mission: "Go and tell the whole world about Me."

But Jesus also knew they would need help to do it. So before He returned to heaven, He made a promise: **"You will receive power when the Holy Spirit comes on you; and you will be my witnesses."** (Acts 1:8)

The followers of Jesus gathered together in a room, waiting for this promise. They didn't know exactly what to expect. They just trusted. Then, on the day of Pentecost, it happened.

Suddenly, a sound like a rushing wind filled the room. Flames of fire appeared and rested on each person's head but no one was burned. All of them were filled with the Holy Spirit.

They began speaking in different languages, so that people from all over the world could hear the message of Jesus in their own words.

Crowds gathered, amazed and confused.

Peter, one of Jesus's closest friends, stood up and boldly preached about Jesus — the same Peter who had once been too scared to even admit he knew Him.

Thousands of people believed that day. The Church was born.

Ordinary people, filled with God's Spirit, began changing the world.

Takeaway: God's Power Has a Purpose

The power of the Holy Spirit is about making Jesus known. At Pentecost, God poured out His Spirit to launch a movement that would reach the ends of the earth. Peter stood up, not to promote himself, but to proclaim Christ crucified and risen. When the people asked, "What should we do?" the answer was clear: "Repent and be baptized in the name of Jesus Christ for the forgiveness of your sins" (Acts 2:38). That's where the Spirit leads us — not to self-promotion, but to surrender. If you've trusted in Jesus, the same Spirit now lives in you. He gives courage to share the gospel, strength to live differently, and boldness to stand for truth. You weren't filled just to feel powerful. You were filled to carry the good news. Because God's mission isn't finished. And He invites you to be part of it.

Reflection Questions

- What's one way you want to make a difference for God — at school, in your friendships, or in your community?

- How does it change the way you see yourself when you remember that the Holy Spirit lives inside of you — right now, not just someday?

- What's one area of your life where you want to rely more on the Holy Spirit's help this week?

(God didn't just call you — He equipped you. His Spirit is your power, your guide, and your strength.)

Prayer

Holy Spirit,

Thank You for living inside me.

Help me remember that with Your power, I can face anything and share Your love boldly.

Fill me with courage when I feel afraid.

Use my life to bring hope, truth, and love to the world around me.

Amen.

Faith Challenge

Today, ask God for one opportunity to show His love or speak His truth.

It could be encouraging someone who feels forgotten.

It could be standing up for what's right.

It could be sharing your story.

You are not waiting to be important.

You are filled with God's power right now.

Chapter 41: Paul's Story — God Can Use Anyone

Have you ever felt like your past disqualifies you from doing something good? Maybe you think, *"God can use other people... but not someone like me."*

But God doesn't wait for perfect people. He changes people — and then uses their story to change the world. That's what happened with Paul.

The Bible Story (Acts 9, Retold)

Before Paul was known as one of the greatest missionaries and writers in the Bible, his name was Saul. Hel was known for something else: hunting down Christians.

He believed that followers of Jesus were dangerous. He arrested them. He approved of violence against them. He was feared.

But God had a different plan for Saul's life.

One day, Saul was traveling to a city called Damascus to arrest more Christians. On the way, a bright light flashed from heaven.

He fell to the ground and heard a voice: **"Saul, Saul, why are you persecuting Me?"** (Acts 9:4) It was Jesus.

Saul was stunned. Blinded by the light, he couldn't see for three days. But during that time, everything inside him began to change.

God sent a man named Ananias to pray for him. When Ananias placed his hands on Saul, his sight returned, and his heart was never the same.

Saul became Paul: a new man with a new mission.

Instead of destroying the Church, he began building it. He traveled, preached, wrote letters, and helped people discover the same grace he had found.

God used Paul — with all his failures, all his past, all his brokenness — to spread the Gospel across the world.

Takeaway: God Uses Broken People to Do Big Things

If you've ever believed the lie that your past disqualifies you, look at Paul.

Before he followed Jesus, Paul was the last person anyone would expect God to use. He had a bad history, but God didn't see a lost cause.

He saw a future.

God stepped in with grace and purpose and changed the course of Paul's life.

Always remember: God isn't looking for perfection. He's looking for willing hearts. He takes your broken pieces and builds something powerful.

When you give your whole story — the good, the bad, the scarred — to Jesus, nothing is wasted.

God can redeem anything. And He can use you — right now, right where you are — for something bigger than you imagine.

God didn't just forgive Paul — He sent him. Paul became a bold missionary, church planter, and writer of much of the New Testament. God used Paul's voice to spread the gospel to new nations and generations. The same God who called Paul has a purpose for your life, too — and when you follow His lead, your story can echo far beyond what you see.

Reflection Questions

- What part of your past makes it hard for you to believe God could use you — a mistake, a regret, a label?
- What would it look like to give that specific part of your story to God and trust Him to use it for something good?
- Who in your life might need to hear how God has been working through your journey?

(You don't have to be perfect. You just have to be willing. God writes beauty out of broken stories — including yours.)

Prayer

God,

Sometimes I feel like I'm too messed up to be used by You.

But I see in Paul's life that You take broken people and do amazing things through them.

Take all of me — the good, the bad, the hurt, the hope — and use it for Your glory.

Thank You for loving me as I am and never giving up on me.

Amen.

Faith Challenge

Write down one part of your story you've tried to hide or run from — something that's brought guilt or shame.

Then pray this:

"God, this is Yours now. Use it however You want."

Let go of the weight of your past.

Your story is not too messy.

God can use it to bring light into someone else's darkness.

Chapter 42: Philip and the Ethiopian — Sharing Your Faith Naturally

Have you ever wanted to talk about your faith, but didn't know how to start? The story of Philip and the Ethiopian shows us something powerful: Sharing your faith doesn't have to be forced. It can happen naturally through listening, caring, and simply being open when the moment comes.

The Bible Story (Acts 8:26–40, Retold)

Philip was a follower of Jesus and part of the early church. One day, an angel gave him very clear instructions: "Go south, to the desert road that leads from Jerusalem to Gaza." Philip obeyed.

As he walked, he saw a man in a chariot: an Ethiopian official, important and intelligent. He had just come from Jerusalem and was reading a scroll of Scripture.

The Holy Spirit whispered to Philip, **"Go to that chariot and stay near it."**

Philip ran up and heard the man reading from the book of Isaiah, a prophecy about the Messiah. Philip asked him, **"Do you understand what you're reading?"**

The man replied, **"How can I, unless someone explains it to me?"**

He invited Philip to sit with him. From there, Philip started with the Scripture the man was reading and told him the Good News about Jesus.

As they traveled together, they came to some water. The man said, **"Look! There's water! What's stopping me from being baptized?"**

Right there, in the middle of the road, Philip baptized him. Then the Spirit took Philip away, and the man continued on his journey, filled with joy.

Takeaway: You Don't Have to Force It

Philip didn't preach at the Ethiopian man. He simply **showed up,** listened, and responded with love and clarity.

He followed a gentle nudge from God and paid attention to someone's curiosity.

He shared the story of Jesus in a way that felt personal. That's what real faith-sharing looks like. No pressure. Just **presence, patience, and openness.**

God will do the heavy lifting, you just have to be available.

Whether you're walking beside a friend, answering a question in class, or praying quietly for someone who's searching, your faith can shine in simple, honest ways.

Faith isn't about convincing. It's about connecting.

Reflection Questions

- Have you ever had someone ask about your faith — or noticed a moment where you could have shared something? How did it feel?

- What are some fears or doubts that make sharing your faith feel hard or awkward?

- Who in your life might need someone to simply **walk beside them,** listen without judgment, and gently point them toward hope?

(You don't have to force the moment. Just be faithful with it — God will take care of the rest.)

Prayer

God,

Sometimes I feel nervous about sharing my faith.

But I want to be like Philip — open, ready, and willing to follow Your lead.

Help me notice the people around me.

Give me the courage to speak, the humility to listen, and the heart to love others like You do.

Amen.

Faith Challenge

Ask God this simple question today:

"Who do You want me to walk with?"

It might be a friend, a classmate, or someone at home.

Look for one moment to share something real — a prayer, a Bible verse, or just your story.

Let it be natural.

Let it be love.

Let God do the rest.

Chapter 43: Armor of God — Protection for Tough Days

Have you ever felt like life is a battle? Maybe it's a fight to stay strong when you're tired. A fight to hold onto your faith when things go wrong.

You are in a battle — not against people, but against fear, doubt, lies, and discouragement.

The good news is: God gives you everything you need to stand strong.

The Bible Story (Ephesians 6:10-18, Retold)

Paul, the same man whose life was changed by Jesus, wrote a letter to believers explaining how to survive the hard days.

He said, *"Put on the full armor of God, so you can stand against the enemy's attacks."*

Paul wasn't talking about real metal armor. He was talking about spiritual armor , the kind you can't see but need every day.

Here's what he described:

- **Belt of Truth:** Hold onto God's truth, not the lies you hear from the world.

- **Breastplate of Righteousness:** Protect your heart by doing what is right.

- **Shoes of the Gospel of Peace:** Be ready to move and share God's peace wherever you go.

- **Shield of Faith**: Block the fiery arrows of fear, doubt, and temptation.
- **Helmet of Salvation**: Protect your mind by remembering who you are in Christ.
- **Sword of the Spirit**: Fight back with God's Word — the Bible is your weapon.

He reminded them: Pray all the time. Stay alert. Stay strong.

God doesn't leave you defenseless. He arms you with everything you need to stand.

Takeaway: You Are Equipped to Stand Strong

Life is full of battles. But Christ is our strength in our weakness

When you stay close to Jesus and put on His armor every day, you can stand strong no matter what comes against you.

You don't have to fight with anger, fear, or hopelessness. You fight with truth, righteousness, peace, faith, salvation, and the power of God's Word.

You are a warrior in God's army, not because of your strength, but because of His. You are already equipped. Now it's time to put on the armor and live like it.

Reflection Questions

- Which piece of God's armor do you feel you need the most right now?
- What would it look like to put that piece on in your everyday life?

Prayer

God,

Thank You for giving me everything I need to face each day.

Help me to put on Your armor — truth, righteousness, peace, faith, salvation, and Your Word — so I can stand strong against fear, doubt, and lies.

Remind me that I never fight alone.

You are my strength.

Amen.

Faith Challenge

Choose one piece of God's armor today to focus on.

Write it on a sticky note and put it somewhere you'll see it — your mirror, your notebook, your phone.

Every time you see it, remember:

God has already given you the strength you need to stand.

Chapter 44: New Heaven and New Earth — Hope That Never Dies

Have you ever wished for a fresh start? A place with no pain, no sadness, no goodbyes?

Sometimes the world feels so broken that it's hard to believe it could ever really be fixed.

But God promises something incredible: One day, everything broken will be made whole.

Everything wrong will be made right. And the story will end — not in defeat, but in everlasting hope.

The Bible Story (Revelation 21-22, Retold)

Near the end of the Bible, God gave a vision to John, one of Jesus's closest followers. John saw something amazing, something that's still waiting for us in the future.

He saw a new heaven and a new earth. In this new world, God Himself would live with His people. There would be no more death. No more sadness, crying or pain.

John wrote: **"God will wipe every tear from their eyes. There will be no more death or mourning or crying or pain, for the old order of things has passed away."** (Revelation 21:4)

He saw a city shining with beauty, full of light, where God's glory lit everything. He saw a river of life, clear as crystal, flowing from God's throne.

He saw the tree of life, giving fruit that would heal the nations. And he heard God's voice say: **"I am making everything new."** (Revelation 21:5)

This is not a dream. It's a promise.

For everyone who trusts in Jesus, this future is real. It's waiting, and it's better than anything we can imagine.

Takeaway: Your Story Ends in Victory

Right now, life can be hard. But this is not the end.

God has already written the final chapter and it's full of hope. You are part of it.

The promises of God are not just for one day far away. They give you strength today because you know where the story is going.

You are heading toward a forever with God where love wins, life wins, and hope never dies.

Reflection Questions

- What does it mean to you that God promises to wipe away every tear?
- How can believing in God's final victory give you hope for the struggles you're facing today?

Prayer

God,

Thank You for promising a future full of life, love, and hope.

When life feels heavy, remind me that You are making everything new.

Give me the courage to live with joy and trust today because I know my story ends with You.

Thank You for being the God who keeps every promise.

Amen.

Faith Challenge

Whenever life feels too hard or heavy, whisper this to yourself:

"This is not the end. God is making all things new."

Hold onto that hope — because it's true.

Live every day with your eyes on the promise that can never be broken.

Closing Words: Your Journey Is Just Beginning

Faith is a relationship that grows, stretches, and strengthens every day you walk with God.

The stories you have read are about the same God who is still working today in your life, in your choices, in your future.

You will have moments of doubt. You will face giants, storms, and broken roads. You will sometimes wonder if you are strong enough, good enough, or brave enough.

But every step of the way, you will not walk alone.

The same God who called Abraham, strengthened Moses, forgave Peter, and empowered Paul is the same God who calls, strengthens, forgives, and empowers you today.

You do not have to be perfect to walk with God. You only need to trust Him, step by step, day by day, heart to heart.

So, keep going, keep trusting, and keep growing

Your story, written with God's hand, will matter more than you can ever imagine.

Final Prayer

God,

Thank You for leading every reader through this book.

Thank You for writing their lives with love, mercy, and power.

Give them strength when they are tired, hope when they are discouraged, and courage when the road ahead is difficult.

Build their faith deep and wide.

Fill them with Your Spirit and guide their steps.

Use their lives to shine Your truth and love into a world that needs You.

In Jesus' Name, Amen.

Going Deeper — Optional Study Track

Bible Maps — Where It All Happened

Abraham's Journey

- God called Abraham to leave his home and travel to a new land.
- Abraham traveled from **Ur** (in Mesopotamia) to **Haran**, then down into **Canaan** (today's Israel).

Abraham's Journey
From Ur to Haran to Canaan

Mt. Ararat

Nineveh

Haran

Mediterranean Sea

Paddam Aram

Damascus
Arabian Deset

Ur

Canaan

Red Sea

Red Sea

Moses and the Exodus

- Moses led the Israelites out of slavery in Egypt.
- They crossed the **Red Sea,** traveled through the **Sinai Desert,** and headed toward the **Promised Land.**

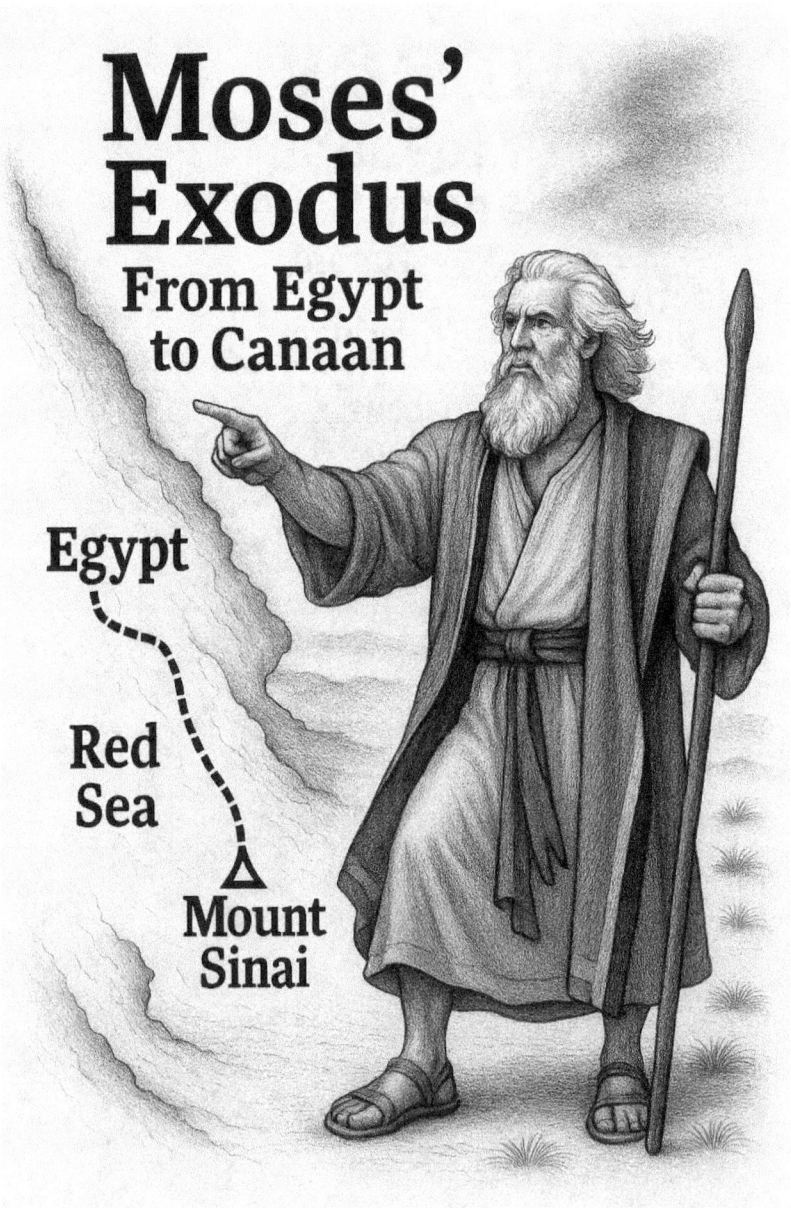

Moses' Exodus
From Egypt
to Canaan

Egypt

Red
Sea

Mount
Sinai

Jesus' Ministry Journey

- Jesus traveled through towns like **Bethlehem**, **Nazareth**, **Sea of Galilee**, **Capernaum**, and **Jerusalem**, sharing the Good News.

Jesus'
Ministry

Bethlehem

Sea of
Galilee

Capernaum

Jerusalem

Paul's Missionary Journeys

- Paul traveled across the Roman world to share Jesus with new believers.
- He visited places like **Antioch, Cyprus, Iconium, Lystra, Ephesus, Philippi, Rome**, and more.

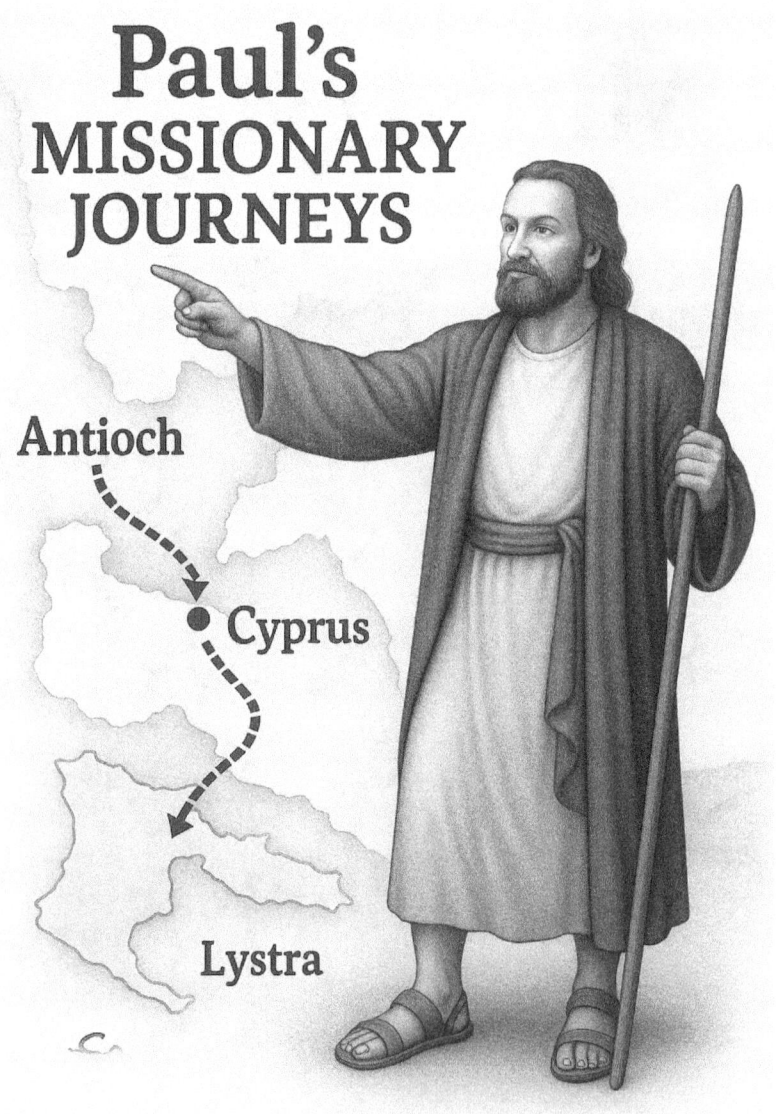

Character Profiles — Real People, Real Faith

The people in the Bible weren't superheroes. They had strengths and weaknesses just like us.

These short profiles will help you see how God used real, imperfect people to do extraordinary things.

Their stories can inspire your own.

- **Strengths:** Brave, worshipful, passionate leader
- **Struggles:** Pride, temptation, big mistakes
- **Why He Matters:** David trusted God when he was young and served Him with a humble heart.

- **Strengths:** Loyal, kind, courageous
- **Struggles:** Loss, loneliness, uncertainty
- **Why She Matters:** Ruth chose to stay faithful to God and to family even when her future looked dark.
- Her loyalty opened doors to blessings she could never have imagined, including becoming part of the family line of Jesus.

- **Strengths:** Courageous, passionate, willing to try
- **Struggles:** Fear, doubt, impulsiveness
- **Why He Matters:** Peter wasn't perfect but Jesus still called him to lead the early church.
- God uses people who fall but get back up in faith.

- **Strengths:** Intelligent, bold, committed
- **Struggles:** Pride, violent past, hardship
- **Why He Matters:** Paul once fought against believers, but after meeting Jesus, he spent his life spreading the Gospel. His story proves that no one is too far gone for God's love.

Key Concepts Explained — Foundations of Your Faith

Some words you hear in church, in the Bible, or from other Christians can sound confusing at first.

Here are three powerful ideas explained simply — because understanding these truths will grow your faith strong.

Grace — God's Gift You Can't Earn

Grace means that **God loves you no matter what** — not because you earned it, not because you deserved it, but because it's who He is.

You can't work for grace.

You can't buy grace.

You can't be "good enough" to get it.

Grace is a free gift.

Jesus offers it to everyone who believes in Him.

"For it is by grace you have been saved, through faith—and this is not from yourselves, it is the gift of God." (Ephesians 2:8)

Covenant — God's Unbreakable Promise

A covenant is **a promise that can't be broken** — even when people fail.

God made covenants with Noah, Abraham, Moses, and others throughout the Bible.

Each time, God promised to love, protect, and guide His people.

When Jesus came, He made a **new covenant:**

Through His sacrifice, anyone who believes can have a forever relationship with God.

"This cup is the new covenant in my blood, which is poured out for you." (Luke 22:20)

Redemption — God Rescues and Restores

Redemption means **buying something back** — rescuing it, restoring it, making it new again.

Jesus redeems us.

Through His death and resurrection, He paid the price to bring us back into God's family.

Redemption is about healing what's broken and giving new life where there was only loss.

"In Him we have redemption through His blood, the forgiveness of sins, in accordance with the riches of God's grace." (Ephesians 1:7)

Memory Verse Challenges — Hide God's Word in Your Heart

Learning Scripture is one of the strongest ways to build your faith.

Even when you do not have a Bible with you, God's truth can live inside you.

When life gets hard, these verses will come back to your heart and give you strength.

Choose your level of challenge:

Faith Builder – Memorize 5 verses

Faith Warrior – Memorize 10 verses

You can track your progress on the page provided below.

MEMORY VERSES TO LEARN

☐ Genesis 1:27: "So God created mankind in his own image, in the image of God he created them; male and female he created them."

☐ Joshua 1:9 "Be strong and courageous. Do not be afraid; do not be discouraged, for the Lord your God will be with you wherever you go."

☐ 1 Samuel 16:7 "The Lord does not look at the things people look at. People look at the outward appearance, but the Lord looks at the heart."

☐ Psalm 46:1
"God is our refuge and strength, an ever-present help in trouble."

☐ Proverbs 3:5-6
"Trust in the Lord with all your heart and lean not on your own understanding; in all your ways submit to him, and he will make your paths straight."

☐ Isaiah 40:31
"But those who hope in the Lord will renew their strength. They will soar on wings like eagles; they will run and not grow weary, they will walk and not be faint."

☐ Matthew 22:37-39
"Love the Lord your God with all your heart and with all your soul and with all your mind... Love your neighbor as yourself."

☐ John 14:6
"Jesus answered, 'I am the way and the truth and the life. No one comes to the Father except through me.'"

☐ Romans 8:28
"And we know that in all things God works for the good of those who love him, who have been called according to his purpose."

☐ Philippians 4:13
"I can do all this through him who gives me strength."